YOU CAN REMEMBER WHO YOU WERE BEFORE LIFE MADE YOU FORGET

How to Transform Your Pain, Redefine Your Story, and Rediscover Your Soul Signature

Janny Juddly

WELBECK
BALANCE

"During a time of global awakening on an unprecedented scale, there comes a book which manages to fuse together cutting edge thinking on the nature of consciousness, the complexity of our path on this earth from both its human and spiritual perspectives, an understanding of energy and the reality of existing in a conscious, compassionate and benign Universe. A psychotherapist, energy worker and spiritual seeker, Janny takes the reader on an experiential and therapeutic journey with warmth, empathy and a sure hand. Comforting, eye-opening, and inspiring, this is a must read. Dive in and let yourself remember who you truly are."
Larry Dossey MD, *New York Times* bestselling author

"Janny Juddly takes you step by step back to your true self, past the traumas, defences, self-criticism and triggers, all the way back to the you who was born divine and perfect. Every page has a lesson in vulnerability and light that might help you through this difficult, wonderful life we live."
Neal Allen, coach and author of *Shapes of Truth*

"… a compelling, thought-provoking and warm approach to the process of self-healing … in line with modern physics. We are much more than our bodies, and we are significant participants in our reality. It is time to move to a new era where we all are healers, healing ourselves!"
Johanna Blomqvist, PhD, physicist, energy healer and teacher and author of *Hyperreality* and *From Quantum Physics to Energy Healing*

"An inspired – and inspiring – book which can really help us snap out of the spell of identifying with a limited, fictitious identity … I can't imagine anything more important in our world gone mad than a book like this – it is real medicine for what ails our species. Highly recommended."
Paul Levy, author of *Wetiko: Healing the Mind-Virus That Plagues Our World*

ABOUT THE AUTHOR

Janny Juddly has been a psychotherapist for over 30 years, working holistically in private practice in the UK. During this time she was also the director of the MA in Dynamic Therapy at the University of Leicester for a number of years. She is also a trainer, energy worker and spiritual life coach.

Known and loved internationally as "The Therapist in My Pocket", she offers webinars, livestreams, retreats and interactive presentations and group work to spiritual seekers all over the world.

BY THE SAME AUTHOR

Dancers Amongst the Stars

Published in 2022 by Welbeck Balance
An imprint of Welbeck Trigger Ltd
Part of Welbeck Publishing Group
Based in London and Sydney
www.welbeckpublishing.com

A CIP catalogue record for this book is available from the British Library.

ISBN
Trade Paperback – 978-1-80129-101-9

Typeset by Lapiz Digital Services
Printed in Great Britain by CPI Group (UK) Ltd, Croydon CRO 4YY

10 9 8 7 6 5 4 3 2 1

MIX
Paper from
responsible sources
FSC® C171272

Note/Disclaimer
Welbeck Balance encourages diversity and different viewpoints.
However, all views, thoughts, and opinions expressed in this book are the
author's own and are not necessarily representative of Welbeck Publishing Group as
an organization. All material in this book is set out in good faith for general guidance;
Welbeck Publishing Group makes no representations or warranties of any kind,
express or implied, with respect to the accuracy, completeness, suitability or currency
of the contents of this book, and specifically disclaims, to the extent permitted by
law, any implied warranties of merchantability or fitness for a particular purpose and
any injury, illness, damage, death, liability or loss incurred, directly or indirectly from
the use or application of any of the information contained in this book. This book
is not intended to replace expert medical or psychiatric advice. It is intended for
informational purposes only and for your own personal use and guidance.
It is not intended to diagnose, treat or act as a substitute for professional
medical advice. The author and the publisher are not medical practitioners nor
counsellors, and professional advice should be sought before embarking on any
health-related programme.

For my grandchildren Lilly and Noah, with love.
May your eyes always see the magic beyond,
and your hearts always be open to the
beauty of who we really are.

FEAR

It is said that before entering the sea
a river trembles with fear.

She looks back at the path she has travelled,
from the peaks of the mountains,
the long winding road crossing forests and villages.

And in front of her,
she sees an ocean so vast,
that to enter
there seems nothing more than to disappear forever.

But there is no other way.
The river cannot go back.
Nobody can go back.
To go back is impossible in existence.

The river needs to take the risk
of entering the ocean
because only then will fear disappear,
because that's where the river will know
it's not about disappearing into the ocean,
but of becoming the ocean.

KAHLIL GIBRAN

CONTENTS

Introduction   ix

The Journey   xxv

1. Forgetting   1
2. The Set-Up   29
3. The Point of Pain   63
4. The Adjustment   97
5. The Crisis   129
6. The Invitation   163
7. Remembering   195

Afterword   219

Acknowledgements   220

Recommended Reading   224

Getting in Touch   229

WHEN YOU HAVE FORGOTTEN...

There is so much more than we can see through our eyes, and so much more than we can feel or hear through our five senses alone. For everything is connected if we only know how to see and how to listen.

WHEN YOU REMEMBER...

Your heart knows what your mind has forgotten. Your heart beats in time to the beat of every other heart, and the Oneness that is everything. You are here to remember who you really are.

INTRODUCTION

All you need to know before setting out

> "Let yourself listen with your heart, sacred soul. Everything you need to know, you'll find there."

Dear Child of the Universe,

Yes, that's who you are. I know that's going to feel a bit weird, a bit crazy. But it's where we must start. Hang on in there with me. It's why you're here, reading this. Right now. It's why you found yourself drawn to this book. You're looking for some answers.

There are no accidents. Ever. The very fact that you've shown up here cannot be, and never has been, random. A whole lifetime has brought you to this place. You are answering a call deep inside that's been growing louder and more insistent for a while now.

And so here we are, two souls on a journey. You have come to find your way back. To find some healing.

Let's sit down together for a moment and take it all in. Gently, no rush.

Life. Confusion. Pain. Joy. Trying. Falling, getting up again. Hoping. Shutting down. Reaching out. Daring. Becoming afraid … That's the big one, isn't it? Learning to know fear. The spoiler of all joy. The one thing above all else that makes us lose sight of all we know; all we've got inside us. The experience that leads to Forgetting. Fear is such a big player in the story. Bigger than you know. It's big because it makes us live our life running scared. We live life anticipating the next painful event, wary of the unpredictability of it all. We wonder where the excitement went, the looking forward. We struggle to remember what it was to feel at peace. Fear wears us down, pursues us, convinces us that the stories it's telling us are true. It robs us of calm, and the ability to think or see. Without realizing it, we end up living a lie and trusting a liar.

We come to believe the Universe to be a cruel place, where awful things happen to good people and life teases us into hoping, only to crush those hopes in an instant. We talk of twists of fate, of life dealing us yet another blow. And we become weary. So hurt and bruised, bewildered and desperate. We need it to stop. For this way of being to change. To discover how to see things differently. To find our self again. To find some hope.

Somewhere an answer begins to make itself heard: it's about remembering. But remembering what? And how? The search for healing has begun.

Then one day you notice the title of a book – this book – and as you read the description on the cover you feel something resonate. What if it hasn't all been random, but purposeful? Supposing there really is meaning to life, and what if it's possible to understand and embrace that meaningful life in a completely new and empowering way? Could there be a different truth? Might life be benign, and might you be more powerful – have more choice – than you have come to believe? And so, something stirs a little. Hope? Possibility? Inviting you to read on. To dare. And as you do so, you begin to hear your Soul Signature speaking to you, helping you to begin to remember what it is you needed to remember all along. To show you the way through. The way out ...

This book is the bridge between the "you" that you have always been, and the "you" that has learned to be afraid. I call the "you" that has always existed, and always will exist, your Soul Signature. It is your unique youness. It is who and what you are fully, beyond and beneath and inside all that you might come to believe yourself to be because of the experiences of this lifetime. Your very Essence. The aspect of you that is always in the cosmic flow, part of the creative energy of a conscious Universe – if you like, your divinity. Your soul, incidentally, is a fragment of that vast energy; it's the part of you that travels through the illusion of time and space, inhabits a body and has adventures.

So here we are, two fellow travellers, each on our paths, sitting talking together about these things, having showed up in each other's lives at precisely this moment in eternity to do exactly this.

"We were always meant to meet up like this, brave soul. Now here we are."

This book is about the process of forgetting and of remembering, and everything that happens in between. It is a book about how to heal. That might seem a little unusual – that link between healing and remembering. We tend to talk about needing to heal "from this event" or "from that experience". We believe that there's certain work we need to do in order to heal the past, that there are specific things we must change if we're to be happy. Finally.

And in a way some of that's true. But it's also a far more global process than any of that encompasses. You don't have an event to heal; this isn't about recovering from particular experiences. It isn't even about changing aspects of yourself so that you can deal with life or relationships in a better way. All of that might be true, in that it will flow naturally out of the process we're going to go through in this book. But it isn't the full picture. It leaves too much out: the core issue itself.

You remember the story about the elephant in the room, and the blind men each reaching out to touch a different part of the elephant, and then being asked to describe it? The one touching the trunk described a different elephant from the one touching the tusk. Just as the one touching the tail differed in their experience from the one touching the elephant's side. Healing is a bit like that. When we focus on healing the trunk, we have no idea just how much of the rest of the elephant we're failing to appreciate is there.

And you are like that, too. The tail, the tusk, the trunk, the body – yes, these are all parts of you. And we could certainly set out on a journey to heal each one. Separately and individually. But know what? We still wouldn't have healed the elephant: you in your entirety. Why? Because we are so much more than the individual issues that we tend to focus on. Those issues are real, but beneath them all, and hidden within the experience of each one, lies the more significant cause of our pain. It's because we have forgotten that we suffer such a sense of lack, of loneliness. Of dissatisfaction. Of confusion and doubt.

So this book isn't like many self-help books you will read. It's no better or worse, it's simply different. It's going to offer you a different way. We're going to look at how to heal *all* you are, not parts of who you are. This is entirely achievable – and I should know, because I've accompanied so many on this same journey back to wholeness, from all walks of life and all over the world, for many years now. The purpose of this book is to heal all you've lost or forgotten; and to do so, you must remember who you really are. That means who you were before you came here, and who you have always been. And once you do remember, there'll be no stopping you!

WHAT I CAN OFFER AND WHY

Who am I and why would you think I have anything to offer? Good question. When you have learned not to trust, not to jump on to yet another bandwagon, or to allow yourself to be tempted once again by someone promising yet another magic cure that will fix everything, why wouldn't you want to know those things?

My name is Janny Juddly, and I'm a holistic psychotherapist, energy healer and reiki master. Before that, I was a university lecturer and course director teaching psychotherapists in training, and before that I was a teacher of English and drama. I've been helping others to find space and healing for over 30 years. I'm also a spiritual seeker on a journey and an adventure, just like you. The combination of those things is what others find helpful. It allows me to offer insights, expertise and experience in a big picture way. People the world over know me as "The Therapist in my Pocket". Strange title, I know, but it arose in a significant way. It grew out of what clients would say to me often when they were facing a challenging situation: "It's like I've got you in my pocket, guiding and strengthening me. I can hear your voice and what you'd say." Or they'd come back excited and glowing and tell me that having me in their pocket had made a huge difference.

It's also, of course, an accurate description of what I carry with me into every encounter or situation in life: the knowledge, wisdom, steadiness and courage that comes from doing what I do. I've had some amazing, startling and profound experiences of my own during my 60-odd years, together with much that's been challenging and painful and frightening. So it helps that I've known these places too. That's our bond and connection. I've been where you are, and I know without a trace of doubt that we can get to the other side.

These years living and working, every single encounter I've had with a fellow human being has left me in awe of each and every one of us. Our resilience and resourcefulness, all we have inside us when we are called to face difficult situations, to grapple and grow, endlessly inspire me. And have convinced me time and again that we are way more than we might think. That's true of you too. The fact that you're reading this proves that, doesn't it? You haven't given up.

> "You are here to remember everything you have forgotten. You are so much more than you think."

Over the years, I've observed the way that this journey we call Life goes. I've noticed that there are key stages, must-have experiences, key moments that happen to every single one of us. It has become the foundation of the way I now help others to heal. Oh, and it feels important to be clear about this process we call "healing". It can sometimes be seen as something a bit magical that someone else is going to do to us. So let's put that right at the outset. A healer is the person who does the healing. Benefits from, experiences healing. In this case, you. You're the healer, here to heal yourself. My job is simply to create the space and show you how. To keep you company. I'm a fellow traveller just like you, remember.

HOW WILL THIS BOOK HELP YOU?

So back to this book, which has arisen out of the observations I've made over the years about our human journey as spiritual beings. It will help you make sense of all that has happened up to this point, and to go forward informed by a sense of purpose and meaning. In this book you will be invited to identify and explore key stages in that journey as they have unfolded in your own life, as points along your own unique path.

"Once we understand our path, we can begin to heal."

As we go through this process of healing together – because that's why we've both shown up here – you will find that you are being invited to listen once again to your Soul Signature, to rediscover who you are, to notice all the support and guidance that surrounds you. Crucially, to no longer be afraid.

THE SEVEN STAGES OF OUR HEALING JOURNEY

As we travel this part of the road together, I'm going to help you discover, chapter by chapter, the distinct stages by which your own process of forgetting has unfolded. We'll go deep into the detail, laying out all the pieces of the jigsaw, examining how they helped build the framework for your life experience, what each stage set in motion for you, how you managed each new happening, and the choices you made in order to survive and their consequences. There'll be no blame, no shame. This journey inspires only awe for its bravery, its resourcefulness. For the generosity that underlies it, and the emerging wisdom that is its true goal and ultimate gain.

These Seven Stages are common to us all, so will be part of your life path also. They are:

1. *Forgetting*: beginning the process of identifying with physical form and immersing our self in the illusion of time–space, and coming to believe we are separate from everything and everyone we see, with little or no recollection of who we really are.

2. *The Set-Up*: life between lives, our beginning, discussing and agreeing the details of our incarnation and Soul Path.

3. *The Point of Pain*: the event that creates our trauma, repeating patterns and challenges – the themes of this lifetime – and how that directly leads to our losing touch with our Soul Signature.

4. *The Adjustment*: how we adapt in order to try to avoid repeating pain in ways that are both helpful and unhelpful.

5. *The Crisis*: the event or experience that forces us to begin to heal by bringing our recurring themes right up to the surface where we can no longer avoid them.

6. *The Invitation*: the point at which life presents us with the opportunity to make the choice to heal and recover our Soul Signature.

7. *Remembering*: we embrace all we have been through and learned as a soul now reunited with our Soul Signature, ready to live life intentionally, and from the heart, in Oneness.

HOW THIS BOOK IS STRUCTURED

This book will take you through your life's passage from prior to incarnating right up to this present moment. It will answer some profound questions about the nature of existence and fill in some important gaps in your awareness. This is a journey we all make. Thousands upon thousands have stood where you now stand. Thousands yet to come will also stand here. See how momentous this moment is? How monumental? How profound?

> "Where you now find yourself,
> thousands have been before."

Sometimes this journey is linear; often it's circular. Many times, it takes the form of a spiral. We can revisit the same stage more than once, and each time we can resist the invitation each stage offers or accept it. The invitation? To hear the call of our Soul Signature as it leads us ever closer to remembering who we really are.

This book will take you, chapter by chapter, through the Seven Stages. The journey you will go on will guide you through the process of healing by helping you explore and make sense of your life experiences.

I'd love to go on this adventure with you – for that is what it is. I've been on similar adventures with so many other courageous souls down the years and have come to understand the territory well. If you're up for some company and would like us to walk together on this final leg of the journey, I'd like nothing more. I have the map in my pocket.

As we journey together, you'll notice that at various times I speak from different parts of myself. You'll meet the psychotherapist helping you discover the unhealed parts of yourself; the spiritual seeker on a journey just like yours; you'll meet the energy worker and the reader of books and research. You'll meet the life coach and spiritual mentor cheering you on; and at times you'll hear a channelled voice: that of my own Soul Signature. You'll hear the latter especially in the Sacred Space exercises and in the memes you'll find at the end of chapters (which, if you have already come across my work online, you might recognize as being similar to my "Instagram voice").

You'll also become aware, as we walk together, that you too have different voices, many parts of you that you may not even be aware of right now. We keep so many parts of ourselves separate, until such time as we begin to heal. Healing involves integrating all those parts, and their many differing voices, so that we can once again become whole. I honour those parts in you and look forward to listening to – and making space for – all those voices waiting to be heard. What a sacred journey we are about to set off on together.

MY JOURNEY AND MY GUIDE

I am terrified. I'm also experiencing the most amazing joy and sense of exhilaration. I can't take in what's happening. Certainly can't begin to understand it. It's like nothing I've ever seen or known.

It started about ten minutes ago. With a sudden explosion of bright light on the ceiling, over to the right, almost directly above me. It flashed, then shot across the ceiling to the opposite side of the room. It was followed by another, from the opposite corner, then another from directly above my head.

We are under the covers, my partner Nicky and I, peeping up in trepidation and fascination. Not sure if we're going to live or die. Yet sensing, also, that the magnitude of what is happening is enormous.

We've travelled through thick snow, the car slipping and sliding, wheels spinning and losing their grip, for over two hours to get here. We'd been looking for a while for a holiday cottage in Derbyshire. We'd both been working hard and needed a break. From the various possibilities, we'd found ourselves drawn back to this cottage repeatedly. No matter what else we looked up, this one kept popping up in our searches. It felt like we were meant to come here. And it was as if the strange hues in the sky as we travelled, vibrant and intense – almost glowing and shimmering – had seemed to confirm that. And now we are exhausted from the concentration of driving with enormous care, just needing to sleep. Tumbling into bed, ready to welcome rest and sleep.

However, that's not to be. Sleep has become the last thing that's going to happen. Something extraordinary has begun.

One light, then another, round balls of mostly white, but others here and there of green, pink and blue, flashing and streaking across the ceiling. All in absolute silence.

The build-up of energy in the room has been intense. Such an energy of excitement, of joy. I want to call it anticipation. I haven't been able to stop myself from grinning. Without being able to explain why. But the energy fills my entire being – a buzzing, vibrating sensation pulsing through me.

At one point, in a particularly brave moment, I get out of bed and investigate the room. Could something logical be causing this? A sensor? A timer? Something human and mechanical? But I can find nothing. The room is otherwise in darkness apart from the moonlight through the curtained window.

Every time fear grips us, and we retreat under the covers, the lights calm down. Then, as we feel braver and emerge once again to see what's happening, they begin again. Gradually, we understand that whatever this is, it's clearly benign. There is no desire to alarm or threaten. It's some form of communication. Some force. Some energy. Something kindly – the feeling of joy conveys that. As does the way these lights respond to our moments of fear, calming down and waiting patiently until we're ready for more.

This is the definition of goosebumps. Otherworldly, like nothing we could have imagined. Conscious, responsive. And "they" seem to be wanting to connect with us. To communicate with us. We lie watching in awe now, gradually settling into the knowledge that we're not going to come to harm. Whispering to each other, "Wow, did you see that one!" or, "Woah, that pink one! Just there! Did you see?"

And then the lights begin to calm. The flashes become less frequent, then finally stop. It's only then that we see it: the figure standing at the end of the bed. Tall, from floor to ceiling, no features, just a shimmering shape. But enormous and substantial, much larger than a human figure. And as sleep suddenly feels compelling and I find my eyes heavy and needing to close, I become aware that the figure has moved from the foot of the bed to stand beside me. By now, however, there is no fear.

Only a deep sense of contentment, of being held. Of profound blessing. I fall asleep in its energy.

The following morning the entire world has changed. Everything is lustrous and vibrant. Outside, when we look up into the sky, there are millions of sparkles. Both of us are seeing this. Reality appears to have changed; or is it us who have changed? Whatever happened the previous night has transformed our perception. As I gaze in wonder at the sparkles, I can hear tinkling bells, a high vibrational sound in my ears. I want to grin and grin. I know something I didn't know a day ago and I know it so viscerally that the whole world seems to reflect it back to me.

It is that everything is connected. That I am safe and loved and held, just as we all are. That there is no separation, in time or space, that eternity is now. The awareness of being loved and guided is so overwhelming it brings tears, in its sheer beauty and comfort. I am changed forever. As is Nicky. Nothing will ever be the same.

Everywhere I look, I see the energy within. I can see the auras around trees, and I can feel energy tingling through me and pouring through my hands. Everything becomes somehow intentional. Guided. There are no longer any accidents. There is meaning in everything. Everything speaks, holds a message or a sign. The sense of presence is profound.

That weekend began a journey for both of us from which we have never looked back. I have no explanation, only the felt experience and the continuing effects which have remained to this day.

Following that incredible night, Nicky discovered that she possessed the ability to "know" things, "see" things. Her premonitions were unwaveringly accurate. She heard female voices urging her to hurry up, saying we had a book to write. We became a formidable team. We would sit up for hours and go for walks in the middle of the night, compelled to read, discuss, find out more. Nicky became a catalyst, an inspiration, with a mind full of questions and possible answers; we were caught in an infinite stream of awakening. Magical, profound, exhilarating and deeply moving.

I also found myself writing compulsively. Hearing words flowing and knowing I had to write them down. I would work with psychotherapy clients during the day, go to bed, and then find myself awake in the small hours of the morning with more words going through my head. Out of that, my book *Dancers Amongst the Stars* found itself written. It has an energy all of its own, and people still contact me now, many years later, telling me what a startling effect it has had on them. Although my name is on the cover, it was a joint production with that energy.

Several years afterwards, Nicky had a reading with an extremely skilled and widely trusted medium. To Nicky's amazement, this woman spoke of us and of our relationship, saying that we were different aspects of one soul. She said that we had a joint guide, which she had never come across before. And toward the end of that reading, which was recorded, the guide she spoke of began channelling a message to us through her. Nicky told me later that this woman's entire face and voice changed as this guide spoke to us, through her, of his gratitude for all we had been through and for coming as healers. We still occasionally listen to that recording to this day.

Despite all the years in between, I believe that "the book" – the real book those voices were referring to, the one they told us we had to write – is this one. Since being invited to write it, I have been aware of that same energy flowing, that same compulsion to sit and write no matter what the hour, that same tall figure making its presence known once again. He is kindly, but firm and insistent. He doesn't walk, he floats or hovers. And he doesn't speak, simply conveys. There is no voice, simply an inner knowing, truths conveyed without sound. And strangely, there is no need or curiosity to know his name. To know more. His identity lies in his energetic signature. It is unmistakable.

He communicates his presence, and Essence, telepathically. It's impossible to miss when he's around.

While he is kindly, and radiates love and compassion, he is nevertheless someone who commands attention and will brook no nonsense. During the negotiations for this book, when I was unsure whether I was up to the task of writing it, an extraordinary example happened of exactly this. It was bedtime, and Nicky and I had been once again discussing the proposal that had been offered, and whether I should accept it. I was scared, still not knowing if I could do justice to all we had come to understand. I decided to go downstairs and put the kettle on to make a warm drink. Halfway down the stairs, I froze, terrified by what I had seen in my mind's eye. The figure was standing – I didn't need to see it to know it; I felt it in every cell of my body – in the middle of the sitting room down there, next to the kitchen. And he was determined. Turning on my heel, I ran back up the stairs, to find Nicky laughing. She had seen him too, and knew that he was about to give me a talking to! She said he was communicating that I was wasting my talents and that I had to stop doubting myself and do what I was here for! So this, finally, is that book.

The energy that arrived in that holiday cottage in Derbyshire is, I believe, a small taste, a fractal, of the energy we all are. One consciousness taking many forms. As I have felt drawn to embrace that truth, my psychotherapy practice and energy healing practice have changed beyond recognition, becoming focussed on far greater depths of healing, and taking many different forms. And a large social media following has grown around that same energy, which has evolved into "The Therapist in my Pocket".

This is primarily a book of healing. The truths it contains are transformative. And universal. First and foremost is the truth which says, "When one heals, we all heal."

Let's get started.

Love and sparkles!
Janny

WHEN YOU HAVE FORGOTTEN...

Life has felt hard, and untrustworthy. So much has happened that seemed random and precarious. It has made living feel joyless and unsafe.

WHEN YOU REMEMBER...

Now you hold a new truth: that there is purpose and meaning in it all, that everything is connected, and that without you the very fabric of the Universe would be incomplete.

THE JOURNEY

The true nature of being human: what this means for
you as a soul walking your path.

"This is your time, lovely one. You can do this."

Before we set off, I want to share a little more about the
nature of the terrain we will be exploring. Some background
information may help. It's about the Universe itself and our
place in it. Knowing these things will be useful as we go through
this journey together.

WHO YOU ARE

You are a Child of the Universe, just as I am. You're not alone
here. The energy that is you is the same energy that is me. I am
you and you are me, and so everything you have known, I have
known too. In the same way, everything I know, you also know.
Since the beginning we have been, and we always will be. In
Love and Oneness. We are the Universe become human.

When you dig deep, it's all there. You've just forgotten. Exactly as you were meant to forget – and as you agreed to forget, for a little while. That's part of how this human experience goes. But now you're ready to remember. And you've shown up, just as I've shown up, just as we planned and agreed, before we incarnated here.

What a time that was, before we became human. How eager and excited we were, you and I, each busy planning how the adventure of this lifetime would go! In that place where we all beat in time to the One Heart, held in the beautiful knowing of its tender embrace. If you let go a little, fade out of the fear and pain into the stillness beyond, you can still find that place. It's in the space between your thoughts. Always. We'll gradually help you to do this as we work through this book. Don't get scared that you can't feel it yet. We're only just setting out. Give yourself time. Gently, remember. No rush.

WHY WE ARE HERE

We planned this moment, you and I. The threads that were to be your life and my life would intertwine in this briefest of moments, this gentlest touching of souls, so that we would bless each other and be forever changed. Together with all that is, we are the creator of worlds, incarnated here in this time–space reality, but children of a conscious Universe which is breathing us, and which is living every moment in and with and through us.

Just think of that, just stay with that for an instant.

Here you are, a magnificent being of light and love and unimaginable power, a vital and unique part of the web of light and love that holds the very fabric of the Universe together, incarnated here to gift us with a journey that you – and only you – can make. This adventure is uniquely yours, dear Child of the Universe, and you are walking your path so perfectly. You are doing everything you came here to do; in exactly the way you came here to do it. Nothing is going wrong, nor can it ever.

I know it often feels the opposite. That things are happening randomly and make no sense. And that you are a helpless player in some whimsical game of chance. But that's about the limitation that is a consequence of becoming human. We forget all that we know and understand on the other side. Our become-human mind can't hold or process what the greater mind, the flow of creative consciousness out of which we emerge and to which we return, understands. But our connection to that infinite stream of wisdom is never lost.

HOW THE UNIVERSE EXPANDS

Let me tell you exactly how the Universe of which you are a vital part – and of which each of us is a vital part – grows in compassion and unconditional love. For that's the heart of it, isn't it? That's what all of existence is engaged in? Evolving, growing, becoming more. Have you thought of it like that before? Watch every single human being, striving, searching, working it out. Losing their way, finding it again. And notice the events and experiences that bring that about. I spend my life as a therapist doing exactly this. And the longer I do so, the more I become absolutely convinced of the pattern and purpose in it all.

How does that evolving happen? I'm going to suggest an answer to that question. It's an answer that I've arrived at over many years of observation, contemplation, reading, study – especially in the areas of the human psyche, neuroscience and healing, quantum physics, intention and the nature of consciousness – and life experience and spiritual exploration. It's the only answer that makes sense to me of everything I have witnessed, and the countless journeys I have been honoured to share. It's this: we grow through experiencing duality, contrast, separation, the living of illusory stories.

IT'S ALL ABOUT BECOMING MORE

We become more through the individual and collective journeys of the souls who are willing to undergo the challenges of a human lifetime; a journey out of an infinite now into something vastly different: the experiences of time–space reality. That's a lot to get our head around when we first encounter it: the possibility of there being a reality other than this. Even that there is a part of us which is not purely physical; the part we often refer to as the soul. We'll explore the evidence for all of this – and the precise nature of such reality – in much more detail later.

As we both know, those experiences can be brutal and beautiful and everything in between. Often, we experience particular challenges, personalities, experiences – usually in many different guises – repeatedly until we have found a way to go beyond them. At which point, we find they no longer show up in our life. And those experiences, with everything they give birth to, are responsible for the evolution of all. It's why I chose to come here, and you are here too. It has been a generous and loving act.

If that feels challenging, let's ask a question that might help. How can we grow in love unless we have known what it is to feel the suffering that is hate, to struggle through shame, to feel the awful pain of jealousy? And, by growing through them, to find a place of understanding and forgiveness? How else does a loving Universe become ever more? How does a soul – for that's who we really are – continue to evolve? And if that soul is a part of a greater consciousness, the creative force of the Universe itself, then that soul's journey must inevitably affect the whole – since everything is connected and interconnected.

"You are so much stronger, braver, older and wiser than you have believed."

Only the bravest of us come for the adventure and the gift, dear Child of the Universe. Only the strongest, the oldest souls do what you are doing. And what I am doing too.

First, though, we need to fully commit to the experience we have come for. We pack our suitcase, jump into the birth canal, and become form. We choose to incarnate. Courageously and eagerly, we arrive ready for the experiences that will shape and challenge and grow us.

HOW IT ALL WORKS

For the first little while, we retain an awareness of both realities. Young children often have memories of where they were prior to incarnation, and if you watch a baby, it is clear they don't yet know they are separate. Then, after a few weeks to acclimatize, we experience the onset of amnesia – what is often called "the Veil". We begin to forget. We no longer know who we are, or why we came. We become fully immersed in our human experience, but never cease to be divine. And all the while, with every step we take, every breath we breathe, we are surrounded by more light and love, help and support, guidance and encouragement from the Universe than we can begin to imagine from this place of forgetting.

We never make this journey alone. We're cheered on at every turn, and we are constantly receiving signs of love and help if we have our eyes open and will only look. It's in that place of stillness between our thoughts, and in the synchronicities that are always happening. This book will help you remember some of those, and help you understand how and why they happened.

And when our journey is done, we go back home. To so much love and tender care, excited welcome and congratulations, so much appreciation and gratitude for the amazing gift we have given, the lessons we have shared, the expansion in compassion and unconditional love that has happened as the direct result of this lifetime we have lived.

TWO TASKS

And so, precious Child of the Universe, we have two tasks to accomplish together.

One is to help you to remember who you really are. Not who you seem to be, from this human perspective, but who you really are: a magnificent and all-powerful incarnation, here to become perfectly imperfect for a while. A Child of the Universe. That is, to reconnect with your Soul Signature, your unique vibrational Essence. The you that has always been and will always be.

The second is to help you to forgive yourself for forgetting. We beat ourselves up so much for forgetting, for our humanness, for the things we believe we've got wrong, the mistakes we think we've made. And all the while, what we've been doing is walking our path, faithfully and bravely, exactly as we've agreed.

We need to make proper sense of the journey, its different stages and elements, from both the perspective of you the human being, who is living this human journey; from the perspective of the soul, the part of you that travels through time and space having human experiences; and from that of your Soul Signature, which is who you fully are, so we can integrate them in a way that brings understanding and context. Achieving these two tasks – making sense of our experiences, and then integrating them into the bigger picture – is the basis of all healing. The two go together and give our experiences a clarity and a purpose we can settle into, and feel at peace with.

"Everything has happened exactly as it was meant to. Nothing has ever been going wrong."

We're going to look together at some key points in your life, crisis points and turning points, the foundations that created the story of this lifetime, the major players, the points of pain, choice, and decision, the points of invitation and softening and possibility.

We're going to do this first in the context of this human experience, which understandably feels all-consuming right now. That fact alone means the time is right, and you are ready. We're going to take this steadily because we want to lay a strong foundation. As we go further, we'll bring in those other two aspects I mentioned earlier – your journey in the broader context of you as a soul, and the Soul Signature you uniquely are.

Let's go back to the very beginning – before this current journey even began. Before there was even going to be a journey. To the Oneness beyond. I'm going to suggest at this point that even the concept of a starting point, a certain number of years ago, in a particular place, in a specific setting, belongs within a human construct: that of Time and Space. It conveys the idea of a linear reality, with a beginning, a middle and an end. The truth is:

"Time and Space and Identity are just a construct."

Let it sink in, become a little more comfortable – the notion that these might only be a construct. A way of describing the felt experience of living a human life. Of making reality manageable, measurable. Meaningful, even. How do we know how old we are unless we know when we were born? And what about our heritage if we don't know where we originate from? Can we begin to think about who we are if we don't have a name? An identity?

Don't we need to be able to place ourselves in a context? To be able to figure out where we belong? Doesn't everyone require that basic knowledge? To understand their roots? Surely no one can exist in isolation? What a terrifying thought.

And yes, it is a bewildering prospect when we have learned to identify with form. When we have come to believe that we are this body and exist in this place. To identify so completely with what has happened to us, and with what we think and feel, that we find the prospect of contemplating that we might exist independently from this perceived reality disturbing. It seems so real to us. If this feels unsettling, try to hold your nerve.

"It's in moments of stillness or deep emotion that we feel a deeper reality."

Most of us carry within us the sense of something more. It can happen in moments of stillness, or deep emotion; a kind of remembering. Very few of us have not come across individual anecdotes – even if we have not experienced such events personally – related to changes in perception or energetic shifts – that take place when a person is close to death.

NANCY'S STORY

Nancy described a remarkable experience to me that occurred when her mother died. Nancy had come to see me because her mother was terminally ill, and their relationship had always been problematic. There was a lot of unresolved pain and hurt on both sides, and Nancy didn't want to find herself left carrying an unresolved burden of guilt and anger when her mother had gone. The two women had not seen each other for five years. We had done significant work together on how damaging some key events that had happened between them had been, and Nancy was finally able to embrace how complex and unconscious so much that had taken place had been.

She could see and accept her mother's emotional frailty, how incapable she had been of doing things differently. Nancy had let go of the painful belief that her mother should have been other than who she was. She expressed the wish that she and her mother could be reconciled but was afraid that her mother was not ready to forgive.

Early that morning, Nancy had received a call from her mother's carer, telling her that her mother didn't have long to live. Her breathing had changed, and she was slipping in and out of a coma. Nancy set out on the journey to her mother's house with a mixture of hope and trepidation.

She could hear her mother's laboured breathing as soon as she walked in the door. The carer showed her to her mother's bedroom door, then went back downstairs.

Nancy described to me how she drew up a chair and sat holding her mother's hand. Her mother appeared unaware that she was there. Gradually her mother's breathing changed again. There were long periods between breaths. Each time, Nancy wondered if her mother had gone.

Then something happened that she still can't explain, but that she carries the memory of so viscerally that it's as real now as when it happened. Nancy felt an urge to lean in closer. She told me it came from outside of her, as if her mother was communicating an invitation to her. She stood up from her chair and put her head close to that of her mother.

Instantly, she felt herself sucked at high speed into a tunnel. The tunnel was so bright she could hardly see. The light had the warmth of sunlight and carried the peace of a gentle summer day. But the colours were beyond anything she had ever experienced, vivid, vibrant. Startling. There was such love and acceptance, the deepest embrace, she felt herself enveloped in loving kindness beyond anything she could have imagined. It was all-embracing. Total. Completely and utterly satisfying. For what seemed like forever she felt herself and her mother somehow merge.

Everything became still. As if time didn't exist. Then, in a moment, she was aware of time speeding up once more, of her mother separating from her and disappearing down the tunnel at what felt to be enormous speed. But the sense of love remained.

As Nancy looked up, full of so many mixed emotions, she saw that the entire room was bathed in what she attempted to convey with the word "glow". She told me that the best way she could explain it to me was to say that it was "more". Not of this world, otherworldly. She was left in no doubt that her mother was "more", as was she; that whatever had happened between them in that moment was on a scale, and had a degree of significance, beyond anything she had ever contemplated. And she came away with a sense of peace around death and dying, a sense of the whole of existence somehow being connected and meaningful, and of the presence of a benign and loving energy that permeated everything. The lasting effect was profound.

EVERYTHING IS CONNECTED TO EVERYTHING ELSE

In my 30-odd years of working with clients, people have shared so many incidents like this. Nancy is by no means unusual. Traditional science, preoccupied with the seen world, the world of matter, struggles to find a satisfactory way of explaining such phenomena. Yet so many studies are now taking place which are striving to begin to understand the complexity of a reality that is energetic, vibrational, interconnected. Studies into near-death experiences (also known as NDEs) that really listen to anecdotal evidence rather than dismissing anything which can't be explained materialistically, or explained away by the now outmoded theory that all near-death experiences – such as entering a tunnel of light, euphoria and the sense of the interconnectedness of all things – could simply be dismissed by the large quantities of DMT (Dymethyltryptamine, a hallucinogenic substance) released at the moment of physical death are plentiful, and rigorously and robustly researched and documented. They must exclude so much that doesn't fit the premise. Which is, of course, what science has traditionally had to do. Geniuses have always gone beyond, initially being mocked or ostracized before their ideas have become so mainstream that everyone talks as if they knew it all along.

In particular, the work of doctors such as Jeffrey Long at the Near-Death Experience Research Foundation is compelling. Dr Long is the author of *Evidence of The Afterlife: The Science of Near-Death Experiences* and his research spans over 40 years, incorporating accounts from many cultures, and from people of all religions and none, adults and children alike, all over the world. The vast number of reports that exist of people who have experienced being outside their bodies and looking on, and who are able to report activities and conversations that happened elsewhere, not just in the same room or nearby, but sometimes on the other side of the world – and which occurred at the point when they "died" during an operation and were then brought back – leaves anyone reading with an open mind in no doubt that consciousness is non-local and indestructible.

No one who has read Anita Moorjani's account in her book *Dying To Be Me*, or who has heard her speak of her experiences, describing the all-loving embrace that greeted her as she left a body terminally ill with cancer, her soul able to go anywhere and seeing everything – including her brother miles away in India boarding a plane on his way to come and say goodbye – can fail to hear its authenticity. Similarly, no one reading neurosurgeon Eben Alexander's account in his book *Living in A Mindful Universe* of finding himself suddenly experiencing 360 degree vision, his mind ablaze with a degree of understanding of the workings of the Universe, unequal to any experience possible on Earth, and so many other similar accounts, can fail to be in awe of the body of evidence that exists for the nature of the soul's experience upon leaving the body.

> "When our consciousness leaves our body, we find ourselves in a vast sea of love and compassion."

THIS IS A CONSCIOUS UNIVERSE

The aboriginal tribes of central Australia have what I think is a wonderful term for the Divine Essence – "The Eternal Dreaming Stream" – believing that in every moment we are all dreaming the world into being. It makes me think of Gregg Braden's moving description in his book *Secrets of the Lost Mode of Prayer* of accompanying a village elder to a place sacred to his people, where he could access the energy and wisdom of the ancestors, and manifest rain by joining with the creative force of the Universe through all his senses until he could taste, smell and touch rain, feeling the mud between his toes and the rain splashing all around him. How closely this is aligned with present research findings into intention, energy and quantum physics by researchers such as Lynne McTaggart, author of *The Intention Experiment*, *The Field*, *The Power of Eight* and so many other recent experiments into the power of intention.

Research projects such as those at Edinburgh University, for example, found that the participants who were able to manifest via intention most successfully were those who reported that a subjective sense of resonance or of "feeling at one" with the desired outcome was the key factor. Another was the paradoxical concept of "effortless striving". Lynne McTaggart describes this also: the ability to imagine something so viscerally that it feels utterly real in our imagination, accurately and in detail, and to then let it go as if it's already done and live as if that reality is now so. Crucially, the ability to see beyond the illusion of separateness, along with the participant's trust in their ability to co-create with the Universe.

A close friend of mine who passed on a few years ago chuckled when he told me what his favourite conversation opener at social events was: "So what's the most unusual thing that's happened in your life that you can't explain?" The conversations that question produced were astounding. Some were about experiences we might label "spiritual" – the sense of everything being interconnected or of an inner knowing telling someone what decision to make that seemed to come from outside; the sense of a benign presence at times of grief or darkness; a voice in the middle of the night calling someone's name; finding the super-human strength needed to lift a car from the person it had fallen onto; feeling guided to a book, a page, a sentence, a word or phrase that gave the answer someone was looking for ... the list could go on.

MANY MINDS, ONE MIND

Other people, in response to my friend's question, shared stories about what we might think of as being more like psychic phenomena. These included instances of having someone in their mind just before that person called them on the phone, or when that person needed them; knowing when a loved one had died; and being aware of a global tragedy or disaster before it hit the news. Still others shared more general questions: how does their dog always know to get excited when they're on their way home, even though that time is always unpredictable? How do we know what another is thinking?

And what about those experiments that show how once something is known in one place, it becomes part of general knowledge without any formal sharing of that information having taken place? How did someone feel the heat of the healing energy sent for their painful back from miles away, when they didn't know when it would be sent, and how did that take their back pain away? Rupert Sheldrake, author of *Science and Spiritual Practices* and *Ways to Go Beyond and Why they Work*, has considered these sorts of questions and produced some remarkable work into the nature of consciousness, trying to find answers to phenomena we're all aware of – such as how we know we're being stared at – but which we are unable to explain. In his book *The New Science of Life*, he challenges conventional peer-reviewed science to dare to ask questions that can't be answered, rather than proving what we already know.

We all have such stories, don't we? Stories that are about happenings that appear inexplicable within our normal paradigm, and for which we need a paradigm shift if we are to hope to begin to think about them in ways that makes sense. Steve Taylor's research into awakening experiences, which he shares in his books *Wakening from Sleep*, *The Leap* and *Out of the Darkness*, finds similar experiences to those reported time and again. The only reason we fear them is because we can't explain them unless we shift paradigms.

> **"When we allow ourselves to go close to the inexplicable, then we touch the true nature of the Universe."**

I think back to my experience in that cottage in Derbyshire, the multi-coloured orbs and shooting beams of light, the huge figure from floor to ceiling standing at the end of the bed, the degree of joy and bliss that filled the room, the billions of sparkles in the air and intensified radiance of colour everywhere the following day, the ability suddenly to look at apparently solid reality and see it vibrating like a mirage. And everything that has happened since. For me, fear has long since given way to awe. So much has fallen into place, so much been revealed.

When my dad died a few years ago, I was sitting in my bedroom and feeling the utter desolation of the loss of his physical presence. In a desperate moment, I found myself asking him to give me a sign that he was still around. (How many of us do that!) I remember what happened so vividly. It was not long before Christmas, and on my bedroom floor was a pile of presents, wrapped and ready. They had been there for several days, undisturbed, balanced firmly on top of each other and against the wall. I was sitting on my bed with my back to them. In the split second following my words I heard an almighty crash, and nearly jumped out of my skin. Turning to see what had happened, I saw the presents strewn across the floor. Once, that would have terrified me. But now I knew better. I knew more. And I looked up and laughed out loud.

POCKET REFLECTION

What would your answer be if you were asked to share something that has happened to you, or that you've come across, or thought about, but which couldn't easily be explained?

Think about it now. Let yourself go there. Stay with it.

Now describe your incident in detail, as if you're replying to someone in direct response to them asking you that question. How do you convey it, make them understand? Do this as if you're in conversation right now.

The other person is fascinated. Curious. They ask you how you understand what happened.

What do you say? What have you told yourself about it? How do you understand it? How would you explain it to someone else? What, if you like, has been your "working theory" about the incident or experience you've just described? Tell the person listening as fully as you can.

If you don't think you can explain it, say why that is. Explain what gets in the way of your being able to explain it.

If you feel in any way uncomfortable about doing this, don't judge that response or try to push it away. Welcome the gift and allow yourself to be curious and simply wonder why that is.

It's all good.

THIS IS A HOLOGRAPHIC UNIVERSE

One of the most powerful aspects of this amazing journey we go on involves the creation of our story. And not only our individual stories, but many stories. An entire lifetime of stories. A reality created by those stories, which becomes the backdrop to the bigger story we call our life. Those stories take place within a Universe which, because it is energetic and vibrational in nature, is like a hologram. We'll look at that more closely shortly but, for now, let's simply consider the nature of a hologram.

The most remarkable aspect, at least to me, is that the whole is contained in every single part. Here's where it's linked to the Oneness we've been talking about. Take any hologram and cut it into as many pieces as you like. When you look carefully at it, even under a microscope, you will see in that tiny piece the full picture that is the intact hologram.

Dr Vasant Lad, author of *Ayurveda: The Science of Self-Healing* and *Strands of Eternity*, explains what so many energetic healing modalities have always understood: that every cell in the body carries the intelligence of the entire body. This has been confirmed by pioneers such as Bruce Lipton in his books *The Biology of Belief*, *Holistic Wellness in the New Age* and *Spontaneous Evolution*. His research into the power of belief in healing has been earth-shattering in its far-reaching implications. And of course, I know this from my own practice as an energy healer: there isn't anything magical about holistic healing; it simply applies the holographic principles above.

In the same way, any individual on this planet, and everything that exists anywhere in the Universe, carries the whole within themselves. Is made of it. It took me a long time to really understand this. And even when I thought I'd grasped it theoretically, I still struggled to apply it. Dr David Simon, medical director of the Chopra Centre for Wellbeing, and author of *Free to Heal, Free to Love* and *The Wisdom of Healing*, clarifies even further: not only is every single strand of everyone's intricate history, in all its complexity, held in every cell of their body, but also in my DNA and in yours. That's immense enough in its own right, isn't it? But then let that radiate out to take in all experience, all that has ever existed – will ever exist – and apply that same principle. All that has ever been in each one of us, plus all that is happening now, and all that ever will happen. Not only whatever has happened, or will eventually happen, but also everything in potential. That is, that could have manifested or might eventually manifest.

Why does this matter? It means that everything anyone, anywhere, anytime has known, thought, felt, or done, you and I have also known, thought, felt, and done. Everything you find lovable or admirable in another is a reflection (holographic image) of something lovable or admirable in you; and everything you find ugly, cruel, unlovable, or evil is equally part of you. And me.

But it also offers you another possibility, one that may not immediately occur to you, because, as Paul Levy explains so eloquently in his book *The Quantum Revelation: A Radical Synthesis of Science and Spirituality*, this also means that – since everything that exists in the Universe is also in you – you always have access to the infinite knowledge, intelligence, wisdom, power, love, beauty and compassion that is its true nature. And yours. It's your true Essence because all of that is in the energetic Signature that is you. Beyond this pretend time–space reality, where we all get to experience and experiment and grow, there is the timelessness of eternity, of no time.

THE ILLUSION OF SEPARATENESS

The nature of the psychotherapy journey – just like the nature of this journey we have set out on together – is that it forces us to examine our stories. Our narrative. When we get to the end we are changed in significant ways. Notably we have grown in self-knowledge, wisdom and compassion. We don't realize when we set out – just as now – that we see the vast majority of what we've experienced as happening *to* us rather than *for* us; that someone or something outside us has done these things to us. That we have been a victim at the hands of another human being, or group, or set of circumstances. Of life in general.

When we are faced with the research – both that of science at the quantum level and that of spiritual felt experience – we must grapple with a different understanding of reality: that while the *illusion* is that we are all separate, doing things *to* each other, the research doesn't bear this out.

Even more challenging, we come to see that there is a further layer still. We must face the fact that everything we have come to believe about our own story – and everyone else's – is at once transformed when we learn that we're all one energy interacting, creating, experiencing. In *The Quantum Revelation*, Paul Levy evidences the way in which reality is actually far more dream-like and far less concrete than we have appreciated. Making up stories, believing them, acting them out. *But all within the one field of unified, conscious energy.*

It's mind-blowing and life-changing, because it calls into question the way we've seen, experienced and understood *everything*. If we are not separate, we can't be doing something *to* someone else. At least, not in the way we've thought about it previously. And if the field of energy of which we're all a part is conscious, creative, intentional, then even our stories might not be as concrete – as set in stone – as we've believed.

> "We come to realize that everything is so much more complex than we have believed."

We find ourselves invited to view our experiences slightly differently. Exactly as someone reaching the end of a successful psychotherapy journey finds themselves doing. We're invited to look for meaning – because if this has all been conscious and intentional then there must be creative purpose behind it. We find our appreciation of the depth and complexity of the journey – the story we have lived – taking on a different quality. We feel awe at what we have lived through and learned; we feel gratitude for the gift of growth and wisdom. We are profoundly changed. And we are immensely empowered. We know we will live life, going forwards, with a new understanding and sense of agency. No longer separate but instead on a shared journey of discovery. Evolving. Not only learning, but also offering learning experiences to others.

Lizzi describes how she felt at the end of her journey with me:

When I started out, I just felt wounded. All I could see was my own hurt. I didn't feel good enough, and I put that down unequivocally to my dad never really seeing me. I've gone through my whole life up to this point re-enacting that same hurt with every man I've ever got together with, playing out the pain again and again. And always believing it was them.

The relief of understanding, finally, that those I experienced as causing me pain came with their own pain, that it was all so much more complex and interconnected than I could have begun to appreciate, has been enormous. I would say it has healed me. For the first time in my life, I feel whole.

I know that I will live my life carrying that understanding now. We are all in pain; and it's that pain that leads us to cause others pain. The stories we have lived produce the stories we continue to live. It's a cycle of pain. I never realized that before.

It's also shown me that someone needs to break that cycle. To own their pain instead of acting it out. And to do that we have to become conscious and aware. We have to see our common humanity, and the fundamental goodness beneath the pain and hurt. That we've caused hurt, too.

If there's one thing above all else I've learned, it's exactly that: we need to see the goodness under the behaviour, the pain that obscures it.

It's not easy, at first, when we're raw and blinded by our pain and hurt, to even begin to contemplate a bigger picture. We just need our story to be heard and understood, accepted fully in the way we see it. And that's okay. More than okay, it's necessary. That's where healing begins: being heard.

POCKET REFLECTION

Think about your own story.

If you experience a reaction to the idea of it being a story, don't push that reaction away or judge this. Just be curious. Notice why that is. What does it tell you?

What events have happened in your life that you blame someone else for? Who has behaved badly? Betrayed you? Hurt you or caused you damage? Been an unhelpful influence?

Do you talk about these events or people with others? If not, why is that? Are you afraid of being judged? That they won't believe you? Or understand?

If you do tell others, what do you tend to say? Are there any familiar words or phrases? Let yourself notice whether the way you describe what happened, or how you describe this person, tends to be the same each time or changes when you tell others about it.

As you think about your story now, are there any parts of it you might look at differently? You don't have to do so, certainly not right now; simply be aware of those parts.

SETTING OUT ON THE JOURNEY

Healing journeys are complex. They invite us to examine parts of ourselves and our experience – our beliefs and assumptions, our projections and triggers. Although this is ultimately gloriously freeing, such a journey is never easy. It engages us in a degree of exploration that can feel daunting at times. Therefore, we need to consider how we're going to look after ourselves while we travel the road we've chosen to travel.

To reassure you again, I've accompanied countless souls on journeys like the one you're about to embark on. You're not travelling alone; I'll be with you every step of the way. I know the terrain well, the mountains and lowlands, the places we can get lost if we don't keep our eyes on the map. And I also know how incredible it feels when you get to the end and look back. The sense of achievement, the pride and sense of resilience and growth we all experience. The way the entire landscape of the world – of reality itself – is changed forever.

PROVISIONS

Just as with any journey we plan to make, it helps to pack a few provisions. I'll carry the map, and the compass, and make sure we stay on the right track. There are, however, certain things it will be helpful for you to keep in your rucksack. I'm going to give you a tick list below of the qualities you should bring with you, so you can refer to them whenever you wish:

Curiosity: try to meet each new twist and turn in the road with the same curiosity as any traveller visiting a new place.
Openness: be as non-defensive as you can; there's no judgement here, simply an invitation to do the healing work.
Kindness: try to maintain an attitude of kindness, toward others in your journey, but especially toward yourself.

Acceptance: everything that has happened is meant to have happened, so there is no need for blame or shame; try to see the gift of growth and wisdom that is being offered rather than the pain that was caused.

There are two further things you'll need to always have with you. One is physical: your Healing Journal; the other is within you: your Sacred Space.

YOUR HEALING JOURNAL

If you've already discovered how powerful sharing your thoughts, feelings, insights and intentions or goals in a journal can be, this will feel familiar already. If this is a new practice, it might help if I say a bit about how it can help you. Journaling is one of the most effective tools for recording your internal process and inner world that you can find. Your journal is your safe space, your soul friend. You can share with it all your deepest secrets, longings and questions, together with those parts of yourself that you want to explore but are not yet ready to share with anyone.

As well as being a soul friend, your Healing Journal is an ally of a different – but related – kind. In that it will be mercilessly honest with you. It will reveal to you when you're kidding yourself, pulling the wool over your own eyes, or being too easy on yourself. It exists entirely in your service. It doesn't shame or blame; it merely illuminates and reveals.

It's also a great place for considering those unanswered questions, things you're mulling over, conclusions you're working on, and things you're trying out. It's like a best friend and confessor, coach and therapist, mirror and champion all in one. A champion because it will also show you your progress, your growth and evolution. You'll look back through its pages and find your entire journey set out there. It will help you celebrate when you achieve what you set out to do.

You can vent in there, cry in there, feel burning shame and roaring rage, puzzle over why certain things went the way they did; share hopes and regrets, successes and mistakes. And your journal will help you grow from every single one.

At various points in this book, I will be inviting you to pause and reflect, ponder ideas or questions, and to take the time to use your journal to help with these. You'll also find some takeaways at the end of each of the seven chapters that follow, providing a brief summary of its most important points. You may like to use these for further journaling. You may also find that there are things I haven't listed but which have jumped out or made an impact on you, and which have felt important. Do please add these into your Healing Journal; they are particularly significant, and meant for you individually since they spoke to you. You can never get your journal entries wrong. Do whatever speaks to you.

"This journey is yours and yours alone. Let your Soul Signature guide you; it knows the way."

Your journal is a therapist you can have with you all the time. (Although, if at any time you discover there are things that you might find helpful to share with a real person who can offer guidance and support, getting yourself the support of a real live therapist is no bad thing.) It's also a link with two particularly important allies on this journey. One is me, because some of what you think about and write about will be in response to questions I've asked you to think about, or things I might have said. Even more important, however, is that it is a direct channel to your Soul Signature.

You will make the link to your Soul Signature most readily by writing fast, almost without thinking, as thoughts and feelings flow out of you. If you let yourself write without censoring anything, not even worrying about it necessarily making sense, you'll find you're suddenly hearing your inner voice.

With all this in mind, you might like to give some thought to your choice of journal. Will you buy one, or create one? Will you explore online journaling apps or notebooks until you find one that feels right?

YOUR SACRED SPACE

Your Sacred Space is the safe space you're going to create for yourself. It's not a physical space in an actual location; it's a space you're going to create in your imagination, and it will exist inside you. You'll visit this space regularly, both when guided to do so in these pages, and whenever you feel the need. It's a place in which to contemplate, mull things over, seek guidance and wisdom, to listen and reflect. Here are the key elements you will find in this space. As I describe them, allow your mind to form pictures that speak to you ...

Your Soul Signature already knows what will feel right for you, where you'll feel most comfortable and at home. Allow your Sacred Space to appear in your imagination; your intuition will show you what you need. Ignore any negative voices that might be telling you that you can't do this. Simply allow this space to emerge in your mind. Don't push it away. Trust and let it form.

Your Sacred Space can either be:

- *Inside*: a building, a monument you can enter; or
- *Outside*: a place in nature, in whatever setting you choose

From your Sacred Space, as and when I invite you to go there, or as you choose, you will be able to explore in three directions:

1. Staying on the same floor of the building, or on the same level in your natural surroundings, you will be able to visit any event, person or situation in your life – past, present or future.

2. If you walk higher – up the stairs, or up to higher ground, you will be able to meet:
   - Your guides or ascended masters: wiser beings who can share greater wisdom with you
   - The Soul Signatures – or "Higher Selves" – of everyone you've ever known or heard about. These can be people currently incarnated, people who have passed on, or ancestors you've never met

3. If you walk lower – to the basement in a building or to a lower level in your natural surroundings – you will meet there the disowned parts of yourself, those memories or personal traits that bring shame, or which you don't want to look at. They are waiting for you to accept and forgive them.

Your Sacred Space will also have an altar. The term "altar" has certain connotations, so it feels important to clarify what this signifies here. In our context, the word altar carries no religious or magical or supernatural overtones. An altar is merely a structure – of any size and any design – upon which we place symbolic or treasured items that hold meaning for us. Its purpose is to help us focus our attention on those items and their significance for us.

Again, this altar will be created in your imagination, wherever you have chosen to imagine your Sacred Space. Creating this Space, and its various elements, in our imagination may sound a little disconcerting for some of us. That's simply because we're used to creating through thinking, with our mind. This is different, and so much easier. You're going into your heart space, the part of you that houses your intuition, and it already knows what will speak to you. Don't try, don't make this a task or piece of work. Just let go, breathe calmly until stillness finds you, and then let yourself notice what pictures and feelings emerge. Then go with them, journey into them. Everything you need is already there inside you. You can't get this wrong.

On this altar, you will place symbolic items that hold meaning for you. These might include:

- Photos or other items reminding you of specific events or times
- Reminders of why you're making this journey
- Specific goals or affirmations that are meaningful to you
- Artwork, poetry, quotes that speak to you
- Candles, statues, sacred items meaningful to you

At the foot of the altar, you're going to lay all your burdens, everything you currently want to leave behind, or to be rid of. You may find, as your journey progresses, that you move some of these onto the altar itself, while some you will leave behind forever.

In the chapters to come, I will be inviting you to visit your Sacred Space for specific purposes. You might find it helpful to record these visualizations and then play them back when you carry out the exercise with your eyes closed.

RECONNECTING WITH YOUR SOUL SIGNATURE

Your Soul Signature is the part of you that is your core Essence. Far more than simply being your authentic self, it's who you are beyond time and space. It guides you, supports you and is always present, whispering truths you have forgotten. It is on this journey with you; you can never be separate. Within the stream of consciousness that holds everything in the tenderest embrace, your individual Soul Signature is uniquely recognizable; it is what you truly are. And so, through this book, but also through your journal, it will be constantly guiding you. You will feel it communicating energetically through the sensations in your body; you will recognize its messages in synchronicities and dreams, in nature, in moments which are deeply emotional. It's there in stillness and in darkness. It radiates a luminosity which can be seen, and emits a vibration which can be felt.

These, then, are your provisions and, used well, they will help you enormously as we travel this road to healing together. Before we finally create your Sacred Space and the altar it contains, let's just remind you once more who you are. It will help you further in choosing how you visualize them and the meaning you give them.

> "Your unique Soul Signature emits a luminosity and frequency which is recognizable throughout the Universe as you."

WHO ARE YOU?

The most important insight in our healing journey is remembering who is walking the journey. So a reminder: you are part of a conscious Universe; a spiritual being existing in eternity who has temporarily become human. You've done so voluntarily to experience life in the illusory reality we know as time and space. Beyond the illusion of being human, you are always connected to the infinite intelligence of every other aspect of the one Universal Consciousness, in intimate communion with that energy throughout. At no time can you be disconnected from this; you can only forget that you are one with everything else.

YOU ARE THE NOTICER

You are the noticer: this means that, at the core of your being, you are pure consciousness. You are aware – observing, noticing. You experience but are also able to be aware of all that you are experiencing. You are the noticer, not the thing you are noticing. For our purpose, understanding this is crucial. It empowers you to do the work needed to heal. To step back, reconnect with your Soul Signature. The Essence that you really are.

As you journey with me through this book, I want to help you to step into your power by regaining two crucial abilities: the ability to notice and the ability to remember. By the end of the journey, you will be a noticer and a rememberer. Those two abilities will heal you, but they will also bring about something else. In enabling you to reconnect with your Soul Signature, they will reconnect you to the fullness of all the power, guidance and support you need to step into the role you came for.

No one reaches for a book like this, on a journey like this, unless they are an old soul, an experienced soul, here on a mission. Turn your gaze out on the rest of the world: how many do you see doing what you are doing? Do you see how rare you are? What is it, then, this mission I'm referring to? It's the mission to become a Light Worker. A way-shower and healer. Because when we heal and reconnect with our Soul Signature, the amount of light we then transmit becomes immense; there's a luminosity to us, and we have tremendous power available to us. To reconnect with our Soul Signature is to plug back in to all the creative power of the Universe without anything getting in the way of that power. To live intentionally, knowing that everything you need is available to you.

If you're ready to set out, there's just one further task I'm going to ask you to carry out. Take your time over this because, as you'll remember, you're going to visit often. Let's create your Sacred Space.

DISCOVER YOUR SACRED SPACE

Find somewhere you can be quiet and won't be interrupted. Choose a time when you won't feel rushed or have a deadline to meet.

Surround yourself with whatever you need to help yourself relax – candles, music, scent, familiar items – and then begin to slow your breathing and become aware of your body.

The out-breath is the calming breath; the in-breath is the focussing breath. Take whatever time you need.

When you feel ready, close your eyes and hold the intention that you are waiting for your Sacred Space to reveal itself to you. There's no need to try to conjure an image up; you and your Soul Signature are a team. All you need to do is be open and allow.

Gradually, you will know where to find your Sacred Space. Let the details emerge, the sounds, the scents associated with that space. Let it become real. You could walk here, sit down here. You know this is a sacred place where only you can enter.

An invisible field of energy surrounds this building or this landscape. It vibrates with the energy of love. It is always safe for you to come here. Spend a little time getting to know it; sit quietly and take in its energy. You are known here. Loved here. Totally accepted and understood here. This place is a bridge between you and everything.

Now build your altar. Use whatever materials you need. To imagine them is to make them appear. Decorate your altar in whatever way speaks to you.

Choose the items you especially want to place on the altar. Take time choosing and deciding where to place them. Arrange everything until you feel completely satisfied.

Now think about what you might want to lay at the foot of this altar. Troubles, things that are unresolved, burdens of whatever kind. This sacred place will guard and keep all these safe until you are ready to deal with them. You can always leave them here. They need never go with you as you leave. Healing has begun.

Finally, choose a word, a phrase, a mantra of some kind – or simply a feeling, or image or shape – which will embody your intention to come to this place. There is no right or wrong choice; you cannot make a mistake. Resist the desire for me to give more detail here. Trust and find your way. Allow and it will arrive. Whenever you speak it, see it, feel it, think it, it will be an energetic intention for you to *be here now*. Those words *be here now* will be your energetic connection to that intention and be the signal for you to come here. Become familiar with this Sacred Space; it is your place of healing.

When you are ready, open your eyes and enjoy a moment of calm before returning to your everyday life, supported by the knowledge that your Sacred Space will always be there waiting for you.

POCKET TAKEAWAYS

- You are part of an ever-expanding field of conscious, loving energy.
- Everything that is – seen or unseen – is part of this field of energy.
- This loving energy – the Universe – grows and expands through the coming-into-being and the interconnections that happen in the reality we experience as time and space.
- This is a holographic reality of vibrating energy which we experience as being solid and real.
- We possess the ability to notice, observe and reflect upon this at the same time as living and experiencing it.
- You are here, reading this right now, because your Soul Signature is inviting you to remember all you knew prior to incarnating.
- Your Soul Signature is the fullness of who you really are, beyond the illusion of this holographic reality.
- You are embarking on a journey of remembering and healing.

WHEN YOU HAVE FORGOTTEN...

What a journey it has taken to reach this place. So many momentous experiences, life-shattering events, have led to this willingness and readiness to begin a search to find out who you really were.

WHEN YOU REMEMBER...

There have been so many years of trying to find a way to feel relief, to find peace. But each one has only resulted in a new battle, yet another war inside you. Finally, here is the way: the path of healing.

1

FORGETTING

Amnesia and separation: how we forget who we really are, and what forgetting means for us.

"That memory is there, gentle soul. You are light and love emerging. Let yourself feel it."

What a strange way to set out on a journey of remembering – by talking about forgetting. Isn't the whole idea to help you remember who you really are? Haven't we already established that one of the reasons you're here is to remember that information?

Fair point. At first sight, it does seem a bit bizarre. I completely get that. So how come?

Well, before we can fully remember who we really are, not only do we have to go back to the very beginning – which is what we'll do in the next stage of this adventure we're on together – we have to go back even further than that. Before this journey even began. Before there was even going to be a journey. To the Oneness beyond.

"Before you took human form, when you still knew what it was to share one heartbeat, and knew that all was one, happiness simply was."

WHAT DOES FORGETTING MEAN?

When I use the term "forgetting", I'm referring to the process by which a spiritual being – who exists beyond the illusion of time and space – forgets the totality of who they are and where they come from; and comes instead to identify so completely with appearance and physical form that they come to fully believe that this temporary existence is all there is.

So, for example, we come to:

- Believe that we are a body, rather than remembering that we are temporarily inhabiting a body
- Believe that we are born and then we die and that we have no existence either before or after those events

- Believe that we are the sum total of our experiences and feelings, and that the choices we make are what define us
- Believe that our identity is based upon our culture, our history, our lineage, our heritage, our gender, our opportunities or lack of them, our experience of fairness or injustice, our abilities and achievements, our talents and interests
- Believe that our worth or value is dependent upon what others think of us or, more accurately, what we think of ourselves
- Believe that we are part of a system that operates independently of us, and that reality is fixed and quantifiable
- Believe that everything that appears to have happened, and that is happening now, is the only reality there is

I mention this because forgetting is something we usually don't realize has happened. Often, we have mostly come to believe those things listed above so completely that any other possibility can sound a bit crazy. Not only may we think that the person saying them must be crazy – that would be me! – but that we would be crazy too for allowing ourselves to even entertain these notions.

BEFORE WE FORGET

Let's pursue some of this a little further.

What do we forget? What is removed from our conscious awareness in the process by which a spiritual being becomes human?

One of the things that always strikes me powerfully in conversations about spiritual matters is that people are usually far more comfortable with certain questions than with others.

While we speak relatively easily about the potential existence of "something more", we're almost always referring either to the experience of the living, or the experience after death.

It's interesting, isn't it, that we rarely – if at all – think about the time before or beyond? That is, we are far less comfortable with considering existence prior to our being born than that following death. Or even, if we believe in reincarnation, the time between dying and coming back.

I understand this lack of curiosity to indicate that this is where forgetting is most complete. Certainly, it is pretty absolute by early adulthood. Experience tells me, however, that babies and infants are far more easily able to remember what existence was like prior to being born. Many Hindus believe that, up to the age of six weeks old, a baby is able to remember where they have come from, and the lives they have lived before. Studies carried out by the Division of Perceptual Studies, at the University of Virginia, have found that many children, from all over the world, especially between the ages of two and five, speak of memories of previous lives they claim to have lived, at the same time displaying behaviours, phobias, and preferences which are unusual in their current context but which are completely in accord with the memories they are recalling. In his book *Return to Life*, Dr Jim Tucker, the Division's most recent director, shares some fascinating studies from over 2,500 such cases that researchers have compiled and investigated together with the late Ian Stevenson, the centre's previous director.

Indeed, I have known children as old as nine or ten able to recall life before they were born. They often share these memories with extraordinary clarity, factually and without any hint of doubt. And they are often puzzled, even a little frustrated and put out, when the adult they are chatting away to appears to have no idea what on Earth they're talking about. Or, worse still, when that adult behaves as if they're making it all up or are involved in some imaginary game.

"When you still remembered that you and all that is are one family, you knew how to listen to the Universe speaking to you. And you never once felt alone."

I remember when a client – the mother of a six-year-old girl – told me how a little girl in her daughter's class at school had recently died following a significant period of illness. She asked her daughter how she was feeling, suggesting that she might be feeling sad that her friend had gone. Her daughter's response shocked her.

The little girl told her mother that, while she would miss her friend for a while, she knew that she was safe and happy because she'd gone with "Yannip". She said that they – all the children – had been aware of him being around for a while, and that they often chatted to him. Just as the girl's mother was becoming concerned, wondering who this man was that all the children seemed to know, and who her daughter appeared to believe had taken her friend, her daughter said something else that disturbed her mother even more. She told her that they all knew him really well, from the place everyone came from. The place where everyone beats to the same heart. She said he was always there.

At first, perfectly naturally, my client had put her daughter's comments down to a vivid imagination, and a way of making something unimaginable more manageable. However, just in general conversation she happened to share the story with one of her friends, whose child went to a different school. Her friend asked her little boy if he happened to know anyone called "Yannip", and the boy affirmed that he did indeed – didn't everyone?

What to make of such a story? How to understand it?

Someone else contacted me excitedly, having read my book *Dancers Amongst the Stars*. She told me she was covered in goosebumps after reading about the orbs in Derbyshire, because her little daughter, aged almost two years old, regularly stood up in her cot in the dark and pointed her finger at what she called "the lights" in her room. The reader told me that she could see quite plainly how her daughter was following something with her eyes, seemingly darting across the ceiling. She also described how, during these times, there seemed to be a strange energy in the room that made her want to grin, and that was a mixture of joy and excitement. She described how her daughter would squeal and jump up and down with delight, showing no fear, but rather recognition and familiarity. She wondered whether these lights might be something similar to those I'd seen.

I think they most certainly were. As well as being an energy healer, I'm also a reiki master. I've lost count of the times a client has seen orbs or bright, coloured lights in their mind's eye during a treatment. A couple of years ago, a client came into my life who was to have a profound impact on my appreciation of energy, reiki, intention and orbs. Her name is Hema, and she has early onset Parkinson's disease. Her pain, muscle cramps and tremors were debilitating. With her permission and active encouragement, I invited a group of healers around the globe to join their energy and intention with mine at the time of each of her reiki treatments.

The results have proved astonishing. The entire group, including Hema, have experienced joint visions of light pouring down into her body, and of bright yellow orbs hovering above her. And during every treatment, she has within moments become totally free of all pain, stiffness and tremor. And she has been able to get off the reiki table under her own steam and walk unaided back to her chair. The effect is cumulative and intensifying. The experience has led to her seeking funding for further treatments and reiki training within her local Parkinson's support groups, and a national campaign for funding for holistic treatments for fellow sufferers across the UK.

How many of us, I wonder, have forgotten early experiences we knew as children? A close friend, on reading an early draft of this chapter, found herself delighted at suddenly recalling sitting on the edge of her bed, aged four, watching coloured lights dart around her bedroom. And when I mentioned this to my eldest son, he told me how my youngest granddaughter, Noah, aged 15 months, stands in her cot now pointing excitedly at what are clearly moving objects in her bedroom. She also regularly waves at someone and is evidently communicating with them.

How many of us live alongside animals – notably dogs and cats – who sometimes sit looking at something moving in the room where we're also sitting, but which we cannot see? Or we may have witnessed a cat or dog sitting mesmerized by something they can very evidently see just above our head, when we are convinced there is nothing there? Exactly like the infant standing mesmerized in the cot in the reader's message.

I recall an amazing happening which involved my son Andrew and his daughter, Lilly. When Andrew was a little boy, his favourite treat when he was poorly and didn't have much energy to eat, was fish fingers cut into squares, which for fun he would be allowed to eat with a cocktail stick.

One day, he and Lilly, who would have been under five at the time, were unpacking the shopping. Lilly reached into the bag and lifted out a tub of cocktail sticks. She showed them excitedly to Andrew, saying, "Look, Daddy – fish fingers!" She had no knowledge, in this lifetime, of those childhood meals Andrew enjoyed on poorly days.

This raises a different question – which we will address more fully in chapter 3 – of how we are born into the families we come to live with, and within which our greatest dramas are played out, in a particular lifetime. Maybe it isn't as accidental or random as it might appear?

WHAT WE FORGET

So back to forgetting. And what it is that we forget? Or no longer see from our human awareness? Experience, reports and interviews with those under hypnosis or who have gone through a near-death experience, current research, years of pondering received wisdom from many different spiritual traditions, together with a gradually emerging appreciation of repeating patterns in the lives of the countless souls that have passed through my consulting room or appeared in training sessions with me, have led me to formulate a response to that question that incorporates some of the following elements.

I would suggest that, amongst some of what we forget, we must include the following factors. It is not intended to be an exhaustive list, but rather a starting point. And, of course, our own individual version of forgetting will be unique to us and will form the central theme of this book as we move through its various stages.

For now, let's consider these:

- We forget that we are a soul, not a body.
- We forget that we are Essence, the creative energy that is the Universe.
- We forget that we are limitless.
- We forget that we existed before this life and will exist beyond it.
- We forget that we are eternal, and have always been.
- We forget that, as Essence, we have direct access to the infinite intelligence of the creative energy of the Universe.

- We forget that everything is energy vibrating, responding directly to the vibrational signatures of emotion and imagination.
- We forget that we incarnate purposefully and intentionally, voluntarily.
- We forget that we are a unique Soul Signature, unlike any other that has ever been or will ever be.
- We forget that we belong to a Soul Family, with whom we incarnate time and again.
- We forget that, prior to incarnating, we chose – together with other members of our Soul Family – the story, challenges, key events, joys and losses, and major themes that we would explore in this lifetime.
- We forget that the specific purpose of incarnating is to grow.
- We forget that this will inevitably involve our experiencing situations and events which will provide us with all that we need in order to achieve that.
- We forget that, prior to incarnating, we formed agreements with certain significant members of our Soul Family about how those experiences would unfold, and who would be central in providing us with those experiences.
- We forget that during this lifetime we will, therefore, find ourselves experiencing conflict and pain, as well as joy and fellowship, with those Soul Family members as if they are doing things to us, rather than providing a context and backdrop, and specific learning opportunities for us.

Before we can move on from understanding the impact of forgetting, we need to look at one of the most powerful effects of that process of forgetting: the creation of our story. Many stories. An entire lifetime of stories. A reality created by those stories, which becomes the backdrop to the bigger story we call our Life.

"Our lifetime is made up of stories, and the meaning we give to them determines the way our journey plays out."

Let's just take a moment to consider one particular idea. It's one that many of us experience some difficulty with, when we first encounter it. It's the suggestion that experiences might be happening *for* us rather than *to* us. It challenges us to give up the idea that life – or a significant other in our life – has dealt us an unfair blow. That we have somehow been unfairly treated.

We have so many complex reactions to being invited to consider that we might carry more responsibility and agency than we'd thought. We spend such a large portion of our lives reacting to the belief that people have done things to us, hurt us, wronged us. The pain and bewilderment of that inevitably circular process are enormous. I remember well tentatively sharing this possibility with a follower on Instagram who had contacted me to try to make sense of some of the things that had happened to her. She messaged me back telling me that she intended to unfollow my page because, while she had believed me to be a wise woman with helpful truths to offer, she could now see that I was completely unsorted and full of "New Age" nonsense, designed to let everyone who had ever hurt or wronged another person off the hook. That it was outrageous to suggest that we had chosen this ourselves!

Here's another example of the burden of distress and the depth of rage we carry with us when we have forgotten who we really are, why we came, and that everyone we come across is actually well known to us and much loved. That we have travelled together down the ages, playing out stories, swapping roles, experiencing and expanding, adding to the ever-evolving wisdom and compassion of the field of energy of which we are an integral and vital part. Ben writes:

Dear Therapist in my Pocket,
How do I begin to get past this? My mother left me when I was five years old. Just five years old! Can you imagine! What mother would do such a thing?
It affects everything. I don't trust people. I don't let them get close. I always expect them to leave. And so of course they do.
And every single hurt just adds to the anger and resentment I feel. I can't be happy for anyone. I feel jealous of other people's happiness or good fortune.
I find it impossible to forgive. I dwell on every hurt, and I replay it over and over again.
How do I break free?
Is there any hope for someone like me?

The misery in that letter is tangible, isn't it? You don't need me to tell you this person is stuck. Going round in circles over the same old ground. Unable to break out of a narrative that has become set in stone.

Maybe you know someone like this. Maybe this person could even be you. Most of us have found ourselves here one time or another.

As you ponder this idea, try to be curious – interested in a completely neutral way – about whatever reactions you found your mind and emotions having. Maybe re-read any thoughts or feelings you have noted in your Healing Journal.

Let me share some further thoughts with you about this. Let's try to make sense of why the concept can feel so emotive. I want to suggest that one of the reasons we find it so difficult is because we have forgotten the true nature of reality.

We have gradually lost the understanding, which we carried for thousands of years, and which certain indigenous traditions still carry, that this time–space reality is symbolic, not literal. That we are inhabiting a reality that offers us precisely the metaphorical experience we need. A narrative intended to serve us, within a world of vibrating energy, which is no more permanent than the temporary human form we inhabit.

We don't know it's just a narrative, of course. A story. We have no idea that this person playing the role of a mother who abandons her child will actually be a trusted member of our Soul Family. That we will have asked to be given this experience in the service of growth and healing. That the experience will be growing her, also.

When one heals, we all heal. Remember?

OUR RESISTENCE TO REMEMBERING

When a spiritual mentor suggested this possibility to me, years ago now, that the things that had happened to me might be intended, meant to be, I was furious. I remember railing about it being a cop-out, that people should be held to account, shouldn't be allowed to get away with stuff that hurt others. Was he saying, then, that we should just let everyone off the hook? That no matter what people did, no matter how evil they were, we should just say it was okay because we'd asked them to do it?

It felt preposterous to me. Outrageous! I remember flinging a long list of atrocities at him, sure that this must convince him of the absurdity, indeed dangerousness, of his bizarre ideas. What if the rest of the world decided to think this way? Would there be no punishment? No consequences? Could everyone just do whatever they wanted with the excuse that they had entered into some kind of mad agreement when they were not yet born and were now held to it, so couldn't change their mind?

It left me livid for days. I couldn't sleep because of how outraged I was. I went through argument after argument in my head with my mentor in my imagination. I felt like a cornered animal. I couldn't decide whether all the emotion rising up in me was because I wanted to scream or sob, run and run for miles or lie down and hammer on the floor. My indignation was looking for a way out and couldn't find one.

As you can see, a big reaction.

As a psychotherapist, I'm familiar with big reactions. They happen for a variety of reasons, but always beneath them something important is happening. A story we have been invested in is always beginning to break down. And we want to fight to prevent that from happening. Our world view depends upon it.

The nature of psychotherapy – just like the nature of this journey we have set out on together – is that it forces us to examine our stories. Our narrative. When we get to the end we are changed in significant ways. Notably we have grown in self-knowledge, wisdom and compassion.

It's not easy, at first, when we're raw and blinded by our pain and hurt, to even begin to contemplate a bigger picture. We just need our story to be heard and understood, accepted fully in the way we see it. And that's okay. More than okay, it's necessary. That's where healing begins: being heard.

However, this really is only the beginning. Feeling heard allows us to consider more generously what other people's stories might have been. Not only how they behaved, but why. The context becomes dramatically bigger: soul interacting with soul, our entire Soul Family experiencing and growing through the drama being enacted. And to which every single player is making a valuable contribution. For us. Just as we are doing for them.

This was the struggle that was going on for me when I felt angry toward my mentor. I wanted to be able to judge and accuse and award appropriate punishment for the hurts I believed I had experienced at the hands of adults who I was convinced had failed me. The last thing I was going to contemplate was letting them off the hook! Just like Ben, I was adamant that I had been inexcusably wronged, and that those responsible must be held accountable.

My spiritual mentor was a gentle man, thoughtful and kind. Certainly way ahead of where I was! When he next met with me, he acknowledged how hard it was to give up our investment in making people pay. Just as hard as giving up our identification with form and all that goes with that. And every bit as hard as deciding to let go of an illusion that has been comforting in the interests of spiritual growth and maturity.

He took me through what I found to be such a helpful analogy that I am going to share it with you here. He invited me to think about what it's like when we watch a movie. A good movie, which draws us so powerfully into the plot with all its twists and turns, and so realistically into the lives of the characters – their flaws and frailties, hopes and dreams, mistakes and challenges – that we become utterly invested in the outcome and forget for a while that it's a movie.

> "Life works in a similar way to a movie, gentle soul. And we are all characters within it."

Then he invited me to reflect on how, once the movie has ended, we're able to step back out of that illusory reality and talk about the movie and the characters from the perspective of an observer who has watched the action from their seat in the cinema. He helped me to appreciate the similarity between that movie experience and the possibility he was suggesting to me: that this life might be constructed in a similar way. Years earlier, in psychotherapy training, I'd read Joyce McDougall's *Theatres of the Mind* and was struck by how similar this idea was, yet so much more evolved also.

It took me many years to reach a place where I could fully embrace such a possibility. Such an immense paradigm shift. But eventually it sunk in. It sunk in because it made sense and because it offered a way out of the endless cycle we find ourselves trapped in. It enabled a depth of exploration, without blame or shame, and a degree of soul healing beyond anything I had encountered before. It not only forces us to take responsibility, but it also allows us to do so.

That understanding has revolutionized the work I do, the way I help others to heal, and the way I live my life. If you allow it to, this book will do the same for you.

You don't have to jump right in. It's okay to sit on the fence for a while. Take as long as you like. This isn't a pill you've got to swallow. It's an invitation to taste the ripple of a possibility.

WHY IT'S NECESSARY TO FORGET

So why do we need to go through all this? If we need to experience what it is to be human, why can't we just come and do that? What's with the forgetting? Doesn't it just complicate everything? Why do we have to lose touch with the Soul Signature we are, go on a long and – quite frankly – often unpleasant and painful hike in search of it again? Isn't that just pain for pain's sake? Really?

Well, try this for a thought:

• If you were a mountain, and you wanted to understand what it was like to be a grain of sand, could you do that while still being a mountain?

- If you were a golden eagle and you wanted to know what it was like to be an ant, could you do that while still being a golden eagle?
- If you were the Sun and you wanted to know what it was like to be a candle flame, could you do that while still being the Sun?

Does that begin to help? And:

- The minute the grain of sand starts to be washed away by the sea, the mountain is quickly going to restore itself to being a mountain, because it knows it can, and because it would rather not be swept away by the tide. It's used to being a mountain.
- The moment the golden eagle becomes aware the ant that it's impersonating is about to be stepped on, it will immediately take to the air and go back to being an eagle.
- And as for the Sun – how is the Sun not going to find itself resisting being snuffed out as a candle flame when someone decides it's time to go to bed?

Does that help to make the predicament clearer still?

A powerful being can only taste what it's like to be less than itself while the going is smooth and unthreatening. The minute the going gets tough, or feels unbearable, or terrifying, or when there seems no way out, that powerful being is likely to call on its power. And even if it doesn't, it would always be aware that it could. Anytime it chose.

WHY IT HAS TO BECOME REAL

The problem with knowing there's a way out is that it means you're never going to have the complete experience. A bit like being in a soggy, leaking tent for a week while knowing that the very instant you decided to do so you could just teleport right out of there into a warm bubble bath with warm towels waiting and some fleecy pyjamas hanging on the heated towel rail ready for you, followed by a warming meal and a cosy fire to curl up next to with your favourite book or the TV.

It's not unlike the actor in the movie my spiritual mentor spoke about. All the time the actor is playing their role, no matter how convincingly, they always know they're on set, being filmed, with sound and lighting technicians all around, and that the lines they're speaking are written by someone else. Even the fiercest of enemies on screen come off set and laugh and chat together as their actual selves again. Incidentally, if things go wrong, they also get to do a second take, or a third, or as many as necessary until they're happy with the outcome.

And so everyone is always aware that what's happening is pure illusion. The emotions we see portrayed are skilfully enacted; the choices the actors make have no lasting consequences; any character development arises purely out of talented script writing rather than actual life experience; any change we witness is confined to the storyline and is a plot device only.

Contrast that with the process of incarnating on Planet Earth, and how convincing our experience becomes once we have undergone complete amnesia. The forgetting is total, and everything that unfolds is for real. I've reflected on this so much over the years, in relation both to my own life experiences and those of my clients. In order to evolve, to grow and become more, we have to believe – and be invested in – the story utterly.

> "We believe in the illusion so completely, gentle soul, that we forget who we are and why we came."

Anything less won't do it. The illusion has to be absolute. Life and death have to feel like life and death. It has to feel like it's forever.

HOW FORGETTING HAPPENS

One of the most moving experiences in my psychotherapy training was the two-year child observation that all psychotherapists in training within my modality are required to undertake. In itself, it is a revelation like no other. The process involves weekly in-depth observation of a child – with parental permission – from birth through to the age of two. No book or video can equal the week by week unfolding of a little psyche from birth through to two years old. It is an incredible privilege; it is also one of the most painful and challenging processes I have ever gone through.

There are so many aspects that make it so. It forces psychotherapists in training to confront, often to re-live, their own early beginnings; it brings back memories to the surface that we have frequently pushed so far into the darker depths of our psyche that we believed they would never surface to trouble us. And, of course, not all child observations are happy ones. We often witness trauma, loss, painful transitions, life-changing events that we know will reverberate down the years.

However, the aspect that is relevant here is the opportunity it gave to observe the gradual process of forgetting. I want to share with you part of a piece I wrote some years ago describing this. It says it the best way I know how. It is part of my observation of a mother and baby:

One thing I notice above all else is so startling that it is quite magical. It is this: this baby does not yet know that he is separate. For this baby, his mother is a part of him, and he is a part of her; they are one and the same being.

You can see this by the way he interacts with her. He treats her body as if it is an extension of his; when she laughs, he clearly experiences it as if it is him laughing, he knows they are in complete unison. There is as yet no "other". As I watch this baby, I realize that he is barely here yet. He is only very newly arrived in this big Earth playground. He is wide eyed and still barely physical. He still knows he is his Soul Signature; he still remembers. He is pure light energy, still shimmering and settling into his body.

However, it is the recognition that he does not yet know that he is physically separate from everything else around him that catches me. The fact that as yet there is no me and not-me. It all just is. I realize that we humans spend an entire lifetime striving for individuation. Yet in this moment I'm caught by the beauty, the simplicity, of this baby's intimate knowledge of Oneness.

And I feel a sudden pang of deep emotion, which is a mixture of joy for the sense of connection with all that is which he still retains, and a sense of the loss of this that he is going to experience as he immerses himself more completely in the life experiences which lie ahead of him. I know that he is entering a world that will rob him of that innocent truth. But just momentarily I grieve for the loss, and in the same moment I recognize that it is my own grief at this loss that I am feeling, and my own profound recognition of the Oneness that he and I, total strangers randomly finding ourselves in the same place and at the same time, share.

I reckon that in the eyes of a baby we see a reminder of who we know ourselves to actually be. We see our actual Essence. Our Soul Signature. We see who we were when we first came, just like this baby. We see beyond, and we remember.

By the time my child observation ended, this little boy's mother and father had separated, and his mother had become severely depressed. His joy had all but disappeared, and he had become wary and watchful, preoccupied with trying to do everything he could to please his mother and make her happy. He carried the weight of the world on his shoulders.

So this is forgetting. When we witness it happening, as I did with this little newly arrived soul, it is almost unbearable to see. And yet it's important to remember that, contrary to appearances, this brave soul knew exactly the choice he had made, the path he came to experience, and the growth he wished to accomplish as a result.

Forgetting happens gradually. It's never immediate, or permanent. It's also never complete. Those who are newly arrived, and those approaching the moment of returning home, move between the unseen world and the illusory world of time–space reality with relative ease.

We are all on a spiritual journey of remembering, and so we are never out of reach of the cosmic flow of creative energy which is our true nature. And which we know intimately through our connection to our Soul Signature. (We'll talk much more about this as we go along.) It is our breath. It is breathing us in every moment. We are forever in deep communion. The conversation never stops. Even when we're not aware of listening.

Oneness holds us. Oneness loves us and accepts us unconditionally. And within Oneness, we play, experience, and grow. Years ago, the Italian theologian and saint Thomas Aquinas coined the phrase "Sacramental Universe" to describe something of this – that everything offers us the gift of meaning, the opportunity of growth. That everything is, in fact, sacred. Including us.

Including you.

This is part of what we forget, and part of the beauty we rediscover when we remember.

It made me smile to read a piece by Richard Rohr, a former Jesuit priest become leading-edge spiritual thinker, who described how a missionary attempted to instruct a group of Maasai elders about the sacred. The missionary explained how it was revealed in those rare moments of enlightenment that come from contemplating the Divine. The Maasai men listened politely, and then expressed their surprise at those occasions being only rare. In their experience, they happened all the time, through moment-by-moment encounters with the sacredness in everything.

The more we allow ourselves to tune in to that cosmic flow, the sacred in everything – the "Eternal Dream World", in which, as our Soul Signature, we are part of what Thomas Aquinas several hundred years ago called "the Cosmic Christ", and which is also known as "the eternal Buddha" – the more easily we are able to move beyond the apparent story of this lifetime, and instead to step into our eternal reality.

So, we forget that we are part of an eternal Oneness, out of which we emerge and into which we re-emerge. We become human, but never cease to be one with the Divine.

> "You emerged out of this Oneness, beautiful soul. You have become human, but never leave the Oneness you really are."

SIGNS THAT WE HAVE FORGOTTEN

What are some of the signs that we have forgotten who we really are, where we have come from and why we came? What characteristics do we tend to display that reveal that we've become so immersed in this illusory reality, this movie, that we no longer carry any awareness of our innate wisdom and power, our uniqueness, or the Oneness of which we are an intrinsic part?

Here are some:

- Being critical and judgemental of others but also of ourselves
- Needing to be liked and approved of
- Being driven to be over-helpful and rescue everyone
- Wanting to prove how strong and self-sufficient we are
- Perceiving life through cynical eyes
- Feeling envious and jealous of others' good fortune
- Being timid and unable to speak up for ourselves
- Constantly drawing comparisons and feeling unworthy compared to others
- Needing to manipulate and play games to control others
- Struggling with intimacy and closeness
- Being quick to feel shame
- Being caught up with the external – looks, age, possessions, status, appearance, wealth
- Holding on to grievances and grudges
- Being fearful of life and of things going wrong
- Regularly experiencing anxiety and fearfulness
- A tendency to see the bad rather than the good
- Feeling bitter at the cards life has dealt you
- Feeling swept along by life without experiencing many moments of pleasure, joy, or peace

THE JOURNEY BACK

So, where to go from here? We've spent a little time chatting together about the backdrop to this momentous adventure we're about to set out on together. Forgetting will have taken its toll down the years, I know. By the time most of us begin the journey back we're exhausted. Often, we're battered and disillusioned. We've grown cynical, hardened. We're suspicious and no longer know who to trust, least of all ourselves.

But despite it all, here you are. A mixture of restlessness, dissatisfaction, a longing for peace and a seed of hope has led you to seek answers and find healing.

How far you've come from that first moment of becoming form, the trauma of birth and the excitement of entering the world. The challenges of getting used to a body – such a different existence from the one out of which you originally emerged. In that place of pure being, to imagine was to manifest, and to focus feeling was to communicate. Knowledge was infinite and power limitless.

For a while, just long enough, you still carried that knowing within you, and the ability to see and hear and feel all who surrounded you and were keeping you company. And who walk with you still, even though their voices and presence have become harder to hear and sense over time.

Then it was gone, and life became real. And in all that time, brave soul, not one second has been meaningless, not a moment wasted. You have always been on your path, creating and experiencing the story you came for – along with members of your Soul Family, whom you will have recognized, fleetingly, without ever remembering who they truly were.

It's time now for us to help you fully remember.

Let's go back to when you were deciding to begin this journey. When you, together with key members of your Soul Family, in the company of the spiritual beings, or guides – whose purpose is to help you to evolve – were beginning to think about what you might wish to experience in the human life you were soon to embark on.

MAKE A PROMISE IN YOUR SACRED SPACE

Using the word or phrase you chose to bring you into your Sacred Space, enter this place of safety and reflection. *Be here now.*

Take a moment to slow your breath, settle yourself. In this place, which is a portal between this reality and eternity, all else becomes stilled.

Take time to connect with the energy that is here. There is such wisdom, compassion. Here you are known and unconditionally welcomed: embraced.

Feel your body let go of its tension, move into ease. Breathe in wellbeing; breathe out into this space until the rhythm becomes one of *being breathed.* All is well with you.

This Sacred Space holds all you are. Although *you* have forgotten, here you are recognized as your Soul Signature. Your frequency is unmistakable. Hold this close to your heart; let it comfort you, guide you, give you courage and hope. *Nothing has been lost, nor can it ever be.*

Let your gaze settle on the altar you have made. Reconnect with all the items you have placed here. Remind yourself of their meaning.

Now, as it arises in you, make your Soul Signature a sacred promise. The promise is already there, you know what it will be. Don't censor what emerges inside you, say whatever invites you to allow it.

Notice how this space confirms that it has heard you. It may be a change in the light, or the sound. It may be a scent, or a colour.

As you prepare to leave, know that this space holds that promise safe, and will remind you of it often. In the sensations in your body, and in synchronicities and signs, your Soul Signature will be speaking to you.

Your journey back to remembering has begun.

Now, or later, share your feelings and thoughts in your Healing Journal.

POCKET TAKEAWAYS

- Everything is energy vibrating, responding directly to the vibrational signatures of emotion and imagination.
- We incarnate purposefully and intentionally, voluntarily.
- We each have a unique Soul Signature, unlike any other that has ever been or will ever be.
- We belong to a Soul Family, with whom we incarnate time and again.
- Prior to incarnating, we choose – together with other members of our Soul Family – the story, challenges, key events, joys and losses, and major themes that we would explore in this lifetime.
- The specific purpose of incarnating is to grow as spiritual beings.
- This will inevitably involve our experiencing situations and events which will provide us with all that we need in order to achieve that growth.
- Prior to incarnating, we formed agreements with significant members of our Soul Family about how certain experiences would unfold, and who would be central in providing us with those experiences.
- Everything that has happened, therefore, has happened *for* us rather than *to* us.

WHEN YOU HAVE FORGOTTEN...

It has been so easy to forget. The illusion of being separate, alone, unguided, has felt so real. It has removed all sense of belonging, of comfort.

WHEN YOU REMEMBER...

But here is the ripple of another reality, a distant memory of a place of love and light and immense compassion. And your heart feels suddenly warm and steady as you know this to be true.

2

THE SET-UP

Love, learning and incarnation: life after death and life between lives.

"You are forever a vital part of the Oneness that is everything that exists, gentle soul. Hold that close."

In this chapter, we're going to look in detail at how the journey begins. To do justice to this fully, we must go back to before the human part of the journey has even begun. To think about why we choose to incarnate, what leads up to that moment, how we prepare and who with, the purpose of becoming human, and about the nature of experience between lives, and of consciousness itself.

I'm sure there isn't one of us who hasn't experienced at some time or another what Rupert Sheldrake, in his book *Dogs That Know When Their Owners Are Coming Home*, calls the seventh sense. That is, the sense that tunes in to the field of energy in which we all exist, as opposed to the sixth sense, which tunes in to the Earth's electromagnetic or gravitational fields and which animals use to migrate or return home. Anyone who owns a dog – as I do – will be familiar with the way an animal can bore into your mind when you're not even looking at them. Or how about those times you find yourself thinking of someone just as the phone rings, or a message comes through? Or when you are standing in a queue at a checkout and find yourself involuntarily turning to see that someone is staring at you? Or even more astonishing, how often do we have a sense of foreboding or heaviness, of something dreadful having happened, before news breaks of a disaster somewhere on the planet?

> "You know you have a seventh sense too, don't you, lovely one?"

BEARING WITNESS

One of the strangest experiences I have ever known, second only to the firework display in Derbyshire, happened on the day my partner's mother passed. We happened to be sitting in a café, and a strange silence seemed to descend. It was as if all the sound were coming through a thick fog, as if reality had temporarily shifted.

I recall getting up from the table to go to the bathroom, and finding myself suddenly unable to walk straight, struggling to maintain my balance. Like trying to walk on the deck of a ship listing in a storm. The floor seemed to be tilting, and the walls were caving in. And as this was happening, the light took on a strange glow, and I became aware that one of the reasons for my sense of everything being unstable was that I was looking into a sort of hologram. Shimmering, fluid. Very much like the world we looked out at the day after our experience in the cottage. Where nothing was solid, and where I felt that if I tried to hold on to anything for support my hand would simply go right through it.

"Many who recall a near-death experience comment on the peaceful silence they move into."

Thankfully, this wasn't the case, and my perception began to return to normal and I was able to walk straight again. It must have been all of ten minutes, but I was shaken for some time afterwards, unable to trust that everything was completely solid again.

When we arrived home afterwards, we discovered that my partner's mother had died that same afternoon. The glow I had seen made me think of so many reports of changes in the light around the time of someone's passing. A few days earlier, we had travelled the two-hour journey to visit this lady in hospital. The light in the sky throughout the journey was so strange – more intense, startlingly vibrant – and there was, once again, a kind of stillness everywhere, even though traffic and activity were happening all around.

And in the hospital itself, while my partner and her children kept a vigil alongside this barely conscious woman who had only days left to live, as I sat in the corridor outside the room her body was in, I became suddenly aware that she was speaking to me, asking me to convey a message to my partner. She asked me to tell her that all that had happened between them had been one of the hardest things she had ever had to do. That she was sorry. Not only that, but I also knew that she was speaking from high above me. Not in her body at all. Clearly free to come and go at will. I sensed when she was there and knew when she had left.

As I have reflected on these incidents since, and have heard and read about so many more, what strikes me powerfully is the way in which apparent reality mirrors or reflects – even demonstrates that it is affected by – the moment of a soul's returning home. It is as if we bear witness to events which, though they might seem to be small, are in fact impacting the entire field of cosmic consciousness. It's yet one more confirmation to me of how the very fabric of this web of conscious, vibrating, creative energy – which we humans know and call by so many names, but which is Oneness – is intimately responding in every moment to all that is taking place within its loving awareness. Everything reverberates through everything else. There is nowhere we can be, and nothing that can happen, that is not seen and known and held in this vast, compassionate embrace.

"The Oneness is responding to you. Right here, right now. Truly, it is."

The Universal Oneness that connects everything with everything else means that we human beings also affect each other with our thoughts and emotions. We can employ this fact consciously and intentionally. I attended a training day with Lynne McTaggart, a researcher into the effects of intention, in London, in which I experienced first-hand the miraculous power of focussed attention and emotional resonance to heal. I have also been part of significant intention experiments in the past where Lynne, who has a background as an investigative journalist, has shown that levels of a particular type of crime, or localized levels of violence, can be reduced by a group of people focussing intentions worded very specifically and then felt viscerally on a specific area. Similarly, anyone familiar with Masaru Emoto's experiments, described in his book *The Miracle of Water* and which prove that human consciousness can affect the structure of water crystals, will already be aware of his astounding results. These showed clearly how water is affected by the vibration of different emotions. When frozen, water that received positive emotion in the form of intention focussed upon it formed geometrically pleasing crystals, while the water which had received negative intentions formed crystals which were chaotic and non-uniform in shape.

I have often joked with my reiki clients that I just need a moment to "plug in" to Oneness, at the start of a healing session. In practice, this means letting go of my human self, and remembering who I really am, in order to allow enormous energy to flow through my hands. I can literally feel it firing up and vibrating through me. And the client feels heat and deep peace. And that happens whether the client is on the reiki table in my consulting room, or on the other side of the world.

POCKET REFLECTION

Take some time to digest these ideas. What have you read that resonates with you? What is familiar?

Think about an occasion when you have experienced a sense of something more. Peace. Beauty. Connection. Oneness.

Allow yourself to be there again. Now. Breathe into that place. Embrace the memory, let it back into your awareness.

This is the you that is in time but not of it. Connected always. You can plug in to it any time you choose. You are never disconnected.

In this silent space, you can connect with your Soul Signature, your eternal and infinite self.

Be there now. In that gaze, where you are always seen, always heard. Forever known.

What does your Soul Signature want to say to you? To tell you? Ask you?

How would you like to respond? However you choose, it's okay, it really is.

Record this in your Healing Journal.

LIFE BETWEEN LIVES

This understanding of Oneness, and that everything is intimately connected, features within all ancient and indigenous spiritual traditions across the world, and many major religions. A dominant theme involves the appreciation of the soul's journey as one which evolves through several lifetimes until the soul attains a state of Oneness – whatever form that state of Oneness might take – with the Divine. The language used may differ, but the central concept is there, nevertheless.

To examine the human journey from a spiritual perspective and to reconnect with our Soul Signature – which is the core purpose of this book – we need to think about a number of crucial questions about life.

Many of us will have considered these questions at some time or another, either privately or in general conversation. Certainly, they are part of popular culture, appearing especially in love songs and poetry. We frequently refer to "knowing this was the one" or recognizing the other the moment we saw them. We speak of someone being our "soul mate" or of having "waited a lifetime to find someone who was always out there". We allude to the sense of someone seeming so familiar that we feel we have "always known them".

Describing other aspects of human experience, we talk of someone being our "our role model" or "our greatest teacher". We sometimes talk about feeling we've been somewhere before, known someone before. People describe recognizing a place or knowing a piece of information, while realizing there's no way they could have come across either in this lifetime.

I remember vividly how my young granddaughter, Lilly, who you met earlier, looked deeply into the eyes of my then apparently recent partner – but who I already knew I had known through many lifetimes – and said, with the utmost seriousness, old soul to old soul, "I've missed you!" It was a moment of genuine and complete recognition, and delight at meeting up again. Look deeply enough, long enough, with your heart wide open, and you'll catch it. That moment when a soul recognizes a soul. It is always profound.

> "Look deeply enough, long enough, with your heart wide open, and you'll catch it. That moment when a soul recognizes a soul. Do you see it?"

HILDE'S STORY

Several years ago, a woman came to see me for help in managing her grief at losing her three-year-old son. As we talked together, one of the startling things that began to emerge was that Hilde's son, Jack, seemed to have been trying to comfort her. Hilde told me how he had always loved visiting the zoo. She had played the song "Daddy's taking us to the zoo tomorrow, zoo tomorrow, zoo tomorrow" over and over, and he had it recorded on a little toy music player in his playroom, where he would listen to it regularly.

Hilde told me how she had been driving along in the car, listening to the radio, when suddenly this song broke through what she was listening to and played instead. She had to pull up and park the car, in shock. This happened more than once. Then her phone would start ringing, and when she answered it, it would be the local zoo they always used to visit together. However, they had not phoned her, nor did they have her number. She kept trying to think of a logical explanation but could find none. And Jack persisted. Every night, the music player in the playroom, which had been untouched since Jack's death, started to play the same song. It would only stop when Hilde went into the playroom to switch it off. Still Hilde resisted. The idea that her son was still living felt too painful. She kept telling me she needed to believe that he was gone. Only then could she grieve properly.

Finally, Hilde and her husband went out for a picnic one day, parking their car next to a stone wall in the countryside. At the end of the picnic, as they were packing everything away, Jack's father spotted something placed on top of the wall. It was a toy jeep, white with zebra stripes. Exactly like the one they had bought for Jack on one of his visits to the zoo. Hilde brought it to show me, tears streaming down her face. "All this time," she whispered, holding the jeep tight against her, "he's been telling me. And I wouldn't listen. I didn't want to believe it. But how can I not hear him now?"

"Your Soul Family are there for you. They always have been. They always will be."

Let's consider what this means. Let's look at what research suggests happens when we die, the process we go through between lives, and how we choose, voluntarily, to come back in a different body, with a different life purpose, together with other members of our Soul Family, to evolve through specific chosen experiences.

DYING IN THE CONTEXT OF ONENESS

Common to many religious beliefs is the concept of judgement awaiting us when we die, either immediately or at some later date. It's a teaching that leads to a great deal of trepidation, fear and dread for many people. It leaves many of us so cold and scared that it's easier to believe that death is the end, than to grapple with the terror that such teaching can engender.

Such teaching belongs in the world of duality rather than that of Oneness. In his wonderful series of books *Conversations with God*, Neale Donald Walsch offers some helpful insights into just how much we human beings have misinterpreted the true nature both of the Divine energy we call by many names, but which I will here call God, and of this earthly experience of ours, all because of our inability to comprehend the infinite wisdom and compassion of this energy. I have found this can often trouble clients since, in their own lived and felt experience, they seem more capable of kindness, understanding, forgiveness and tolerance than does the God with whom they would like to have a relationship.

Spiritual traditions, in contrast to most religious belief systems, tend to embrace a different understanding of the Universe. One that involves Oneness, a field of loving and creative consciousness which is constantly evolving. More in line with the thoughts we've already explored a little. This felt wisdom – born out of direct experience of communion with Divine energy – speaks of an entity vastly different in nature and substance from the concept of an all-powerful, judging deity; and mystics of all religions, and none, down the ages have also found themselves aligning with this truth. Universally, this is the energy they encounter in those experiences we might describe as states of awakening or enlightenment.

"The Universe loves you unconditionally, without judgement, dear soul."

I love the wonderful words that are attributed to the Sufi mystic, Islamic dervish and poet Jalal ad-Din Muhammed Rumi, who lived about 800 years ago: "You are not a drop in the ocean; you are the entire ocean in a drop." Wherever you look, there is a growing movement toward an appreciation, amongst those who are awakening to the deeper truths of the nature of this Conscious Universe, or who have known that place down the centuries, of the Oneness we all are.

THE EVIDENCE FOR NEAR-DEATH EXPERIENCES AND REINCARNATION

In a moment, I'm going to share with you some of the key experiences that those recounting near-death experiences, or recalling life after death, report virtually unanimously, often using the same kinds of metaphors completely independently of each other. Without exception, people describe these experiences with shock and surprise, with awe and enormous emotion. No one interviewed has ever claimed to have expected anything like this to happen, or to have encountered such experiences before.

The experiences in the list below occur frequently in research findings and reports. The first category or cluster of experiences belong to those commonly referred to as NDEs or Near-Death

Experiences, a term originally coined by Dr Raymond Moody in 1977 in his ground-breaking books *Life After Life* and *The Light Beyond*, upon which all subsequent research is founded. NDEs are frequently profoundly spiritual experiences, happen uninvited and unexpectedly, and have a lasting effect on the person thereafter. People who have experienced NDEs commonly report:

- Discovering the ability, especially where death is anticipated, and pain involved, of being able to leave the body at will
- Rising up, floating above the body, and looking down on the body and the accompanying scene below
- Being able to see and hear activities and conversations going on outside the place where the body is, ranging from outside in a corridor and in other rooms, to places in other parts of the world where their loved ones are
- The sense of watching on but being apart, as if watching a movie
- A pulling sensation, like a strong magnet, tugging the soul away from the body
- A strong desire to tell loved ones that all is well, but the grief and strong emotion being experienced by loved ones blocking that communication
- Realizing that they are free, limitless, without restriction, and free of pain or fear.
- A sense of a bright light, and being pulled into it
- Finding themselves in a tunnel, moving along at speed toward the source of that bright light
- The experience of time having a different quality – everything is happening now
- An enormous life force surging through them
- Realizing that nothing is solid, but energetic
- Hearing music or soothing vibrations

- Feeling encased in immensely loving, accepting, compassionate energy
- Being greeted by loved ones

People who recall previous lives, or life between lives, either under deep hypnosis, or – like young children – because those memories happen spontaneously, frequently describe:

- Travelling at speed through the cosmos toward what they realize is a known destination
- This journey being peaceful, not in any way alarming
- Gradually beginning to remember that they are going back to their soul group, or soul family. Often they describe how they sense them telepathically and vibrationally, or as if their soul family is "singing" to them, calling them home beyond this earthly reality
- Souls appearing at a distance as orbs of light, but becoming recognizable by their individual essence (soul signature) as they get closer
- A sense of order and harmony, and a feeling of enormous comfort
- The joy of meeting up once more with people they thought they would never see again, believing they were no longer alive

THE NATURE OF LIFE AFTER DEATH

Let's go a little further. We've looked at some of the evidence that suggests that life goes on beyond death. And that there is life between lives. That there is substantial research which suggests we live more than one life.

Let's now look more closely at the specific nature of life between lives, and at its direct relevance to the work that we are doing together. Let's start to bring some of the various threads together. Why are we going into so much detail about life after death? Isn't the reason we're here, together on this journey, more about trying to heal what's happened in this life, rather than thinking about what's going to happen at the end of it?

A quick reminder: soul healing – healing that's complete and permanent – must be gone through. At a pace that allows it to reach all parts of us and have a profound effect. It isn't an intellectual process. You can't simply assimilate ideas and hope that will do the trick. I've lost count of the number of clients who have said to me something along the lines of, "Yeah, I understand it all, so why don't I feel better yet?" It's tempting, isn't it, to want the relief of the quick fix? The sticking plaster rather than the operation? And I also hold in enormous admiration all those who have trusted me enough to stay in the process until they could feel the change rather than merely understand the principle. This journey is a holistic one, not a merely cognitive one. You really are on your way. Keep the faith!

"Break open, soften, allow – your soul knows the way."

For now, the main truth I want to ask you to hold is that everyone who has undergone a near-death experience has been profoundly changed by it, in a positive way. The understanding that we are all connected affects people profoundly. As does the experience of finding themselves in a sea of compassionate, all-embracing love. Together with a sense – which never leaves them – that all is well.

And everyone who has recalled, whether under hypnosis or spontaneously, the nature of their existence between lives has found that they begin to see connections in their current life they hadn't realized were there. They find that they can see patterns and purpose in everything that has taken place in their life. Random events become meaningful. They begin to appreciate that nothing has been accidental, neither people nor events. Even the briefest of encounters is suddenly seen as influential, with lasting effects.

While what is recalled is often beyond the scope of language to convey, people frequently talk about the immense sense of love and acceptance, of there being no judgement, of having choice and free will. There is always joy at seeing loved ones again, and often the subject under hypnosis will speak of being reunited with those who have played different roles in previous lives. They will report that the person they've just recognized as their sister, for example, was an abusive husband in a different life. But these recollections happen in an atmosphere of enormous affection and lightness. There is no grudge, no fear, no desire for revenge.

"Everything is connected and love is all there is."

Recollections of previous lives, away from the illusions of space and time, are seen for what they are: the stories we live out during a lifetime, and from which we learn and grow. Someone once asked Michael Newton, author of *Journey of Souls*, why he thought this information regarding reincarnation was coming to light at the current time. He suggested that it might be to help us realize that our actions matter and that, since we will encounter this planet again, we should take better care of it and each other. Paul Aurand, author of *Essential Healing*, puts it another way, pointing out that it's much harder to harm others if we know we're all spiritually connected. In his book *When Souls Awaken*, Peter Jan Elsen PhD shares some wonderful insights into the purpose of life on Earth and reincarnation, focussing on the spiritual evolution he sees taking place.

Richard Martini, in *Flipside: A Tourist's Guide on How to Navigate the Afterlife*, talks of the way that those under hypnosis speak about the Universe as running on love – saying that love is equivalent to gravity, being the force that binds the universe together. These types of phenomena used to be dismissed as hallucinations, or even wishful thinking. Increasingly, however, such attempted explanations of these experiences are seen as inadequate because they are incomplete. They can't explain, for example, descriptions of people who suddenly possess 360-degree vision and accurately describe conversations that take place elsewhere in other rooms or in hospital corridors, or who witness global events while bed-ridden. Too much has to be discarded or ignored to make these occurrences fit into an increasingly limited and mechanistic paradigm.

The similarities in all accounts, across all cultures and all age groups, is compelling. In terms of our journey together here, in this book, it is also hugely important.

WHAT ARE WE AFRAID OF?

We spend so much time running away from, and so little time leaning closer to, the major mysteries and miracles of life, death and existence. Or maybe some of us do, but we tend to do so through received teaching, religious articles or dogma, and what others tell us to believe, rather than daring to go near anything that appears not to fall neatly and comfortably within the religious paradigm or particular set of spiritual beliefs we adhere to.

The reason? Well, we could say lack of interest or lack of curiosity. We could equally talk about it being to do with never having stopped to consider such things. Someone dies, there's

"The answers reveal themselves in the quiet moments. Give yourself the gift of time to feel what is true."

a funeral, people grieve; there's a familiar pattern and ritual to it all. But how often do we stop and think to wonder, out loud or privately, "Where are they now?" or, "What was it like?" or, "Can they still see me?"

"Fear makes us dismiss possibilities without even considering them, gentle soul. Don't let fear win this time. You are stronger than you believe."

I have a strong inkling that the far more likely reason we don't allow ourselves too much curiosity is down to our old friend Fear. Fear makes us dismiss possibilities without even considering them. It's fear that makes us mock or deride pieces of research without even reading them. And it's fear, pure and simple, therefore, that creates the true barrier to healing.

So let's give fear some space. Allow it in. Engage with it. Commune with it. Let's take some time to listen respectfully, and then to respond equally respectfully.

POCKET REFLECTION

What is fear doing in your body right now?

You may not be aware of its presence at all. And if so, that's fine. Concentrate, instead, on allowing the sense of calm and resonance to fill you. Enjoy that feeling.

However, if you have found fear there, notice it, be curious about it. Note what it's saying to you. What it's asking you to believe. Asking you to do.

Why does fear find these ideas challenging? Observe this fear as if it's separate from you. It's Fear itself, not your fear. This is not you. You are not fearful. You can step outside and look on at the part that is: Fear. You are simply noticing the sensations that Fear evokes in your body. You are just looking on. The observer. Conscious awareness. You are not this Fear.

So now, what is Fear afraid of? That you might go beyond it? That you might not believe it anymore? That something terrible will happen because you are thinking differently – your own thoughts rather than Fear's thoughts?

Could it be that Fear might even be detecting your Soul Signature? Inviting you to open to new possibilities? Inviting you to let yourself heal?

What do you say to Fear now? Remember that Fear is only trying to protect you, as it has done for so long. How will you reassure it that it doesn't need to shield you from this? That this is part of your healing, brave soul. Fear has been an old friend, but it's time for it to let you discover a new way now.

EXPERIENCES OF THE AFTERLIFE

So then, back to life between lives, and what the growing body of research tells us. Under hypnosis, there are common recollections. These often come from subjects who have used hypnotherapy to try to understand and deal with the cause of their pain or trauma. The same recollections of the afterlife appear with subjects whether they have had a strong religious belief, which doesn't include incarnation, or, indeed, they are pronounced atheists. All recall their experiences so viscerally that they emerge from hypnosis knowing them to be true. Reliving what happened tends to be emotionally overwhelming. In particular, the reunions they find themselves reliving with their guides and members of their Soul Family – not all of whom incarnate in every lifetime – are a source of immense celebration and comfort. There is a feeling of returning home to what is familiar and known.

> "Every life is precious.
> Each lifetime we evolve still more.
> How many have you known?"

Here are some of the experiences people regularly report. They are gathered from thousands of such subjects, the world over:

- In the afterlife, we exist in an environment of unconditional love, acceptance and kindness.
- We all have at least one guide, who normally meets us upon death, together with key loved ones.
- Communication between souls is telepathic, we "know and feel" rather than hear, although subjects often talk of sounds akin to humming or singing, which appear to denote a frequency of vibration rather than an actual noise.
- We recognize loved ones, members of our Soul Family and our guides by their unique energy or "Essence" – their Soul Signature.
- How evolved souls are is evident by their dominant colour: more evolved souls show up as deep blues and purples, while less evolved souls are more often pastel shades.
- There is no hierarchy. Everyone is treated equally. The more evolved a soul is, the humbler they tend to be.
- The process of reincarnation is planned with great care, in consultation with guides and Soul Family members, and with a panel of kindly elders who guide and help us.

- Reincarnation is not subject to karma as we think of it – rather, we choose what we want to experience or learn or grow through in our next lifetime.
- Reincarnation itself is voluntary, not forced or demanded. However, we are usually eager, after a period of rest, acclimatization and healing, to experience another lifetime, because in that reality we comprehend things differently.
- We undergo two life reviews: one shortly after death (in which we look back at our past life) and another prior to reincarnating (in which we plan the details of our next life). These are kindly, supportive meetings with a group of loving, wise elders or guides, who help us to think about our choices and the qualities we want to develop.
- Not everyone reincarnates. Some become guides or healers supporting those who have chosen to incarnate.
- Learning in the life between lives is focussed on learning how to manipulate energy and on healing.
- Our life choices are entirely up to us: sometimes we choose to work on a particular issue that will help us to evolve; other times, we choose to incarnate in order to support a member of our Soul Family to explore an issue they have chosen for a particular lifetime – therefore, our worst enemy while incarnated can turn out to be a close and much loved member of our Soul Family when we return.
- When we return home, all negativity is left behind. Our actions do not follow us, nor do the actions of others. There is only love and acceptance, and an attitude of kindness and an environment in which learning and evolving are encouraged.
- Our animal friends – which are energetic signatures just as we are – join us during lifetimes, but also between lifetimes.

- Only a percentage of our total soul energy incarnates –
  usually somewhere around 25 per cent to 38 per cent.
  It's all our physical form can handle. The remaining
  percentage is always available to us to consult or take
  strength from. It knows our soul plan and life purpose. This
  is often referred to as our Higher Self.

I'm guessing some things on this list might already be familiar
to you, and others not so.

One of the astonishing revelations I had while researching this
whole area was the shock of recognizing that I had either visited
during sleep, or recalled in several dreams, the halls of learning
so often described in these reports. I distinctly recall waking one
morning and telling my partner how I seemed to have spent the
entire night in a huge room, a bit like something out of *Harry
Potter*, learning to make an object lift off a surface with the power
of my mind. I described the mayhem that ensued as I tried in
vain to get it to move to where I wanted it to go – it took many
attempts, and I lived through each attempt in detail, trying again
and again and feeling the frustration of being unsuccessful –
before I finally managed to achieve the necessary manoeuvre. I
also recalled great celebration when I finally managed it! There
seemed to be a ceremony of some sort! I found the experience
puzzling and bizarre, but so visceral I woke believing I was still
there. The dream would have been a good five years or so prior
to my reading any of this research. Absolutely jaw-dropping!

POCKET REFLECTION

How did you find yourself reacting to these research
findings? Try not to judge or reject or cherry-pick
your responses. All are valid. Each one of them offers
helpful information.

Maybe you find some of the points listed above more challenging than others? Let yourself dwell on your response to those. Be curious about the reasons behind those responses.

Stay open-minded. There is no right or wrong reaction, just your own unique response. So much to think about. So many places to go. Take your time. Don't rush this.

If this is all true, if this is how it all really goes, what are the implications for you in it all? Take all the time you need to respond to this. Feel it as well as consider it in your head.

Are there ways this information might help you? Things you might look at differently? Are there gifts here for you? If so, what might they be?

WHAT ABOUT "GOOD" AND "EVIL"?

Before going any further, I want to address one issue that many of us find challenging on first coming up against it. Remember my fury when my spiritual director suggested that everyone is playing a valuable role in our lives, even those who hurt us? It's hard, isn't it, to even contemplate that our worst enemies might be members of our Soul Family?

When we think in human terms, believe that we're all separate and think dualistically, we feel outraged at the idea. We want people punished. Held to account. However, that becomes difficult once we appreciate what Oneness really means. Back to the holograph: inside every one of us exist all of us. While we might not all carry out cruel acts in this lifetime, we certainly all have the potential to feel the intense emotions which lead to those acts. (We'll address this more when we talk about "the shadow" in chapter 6, "The Invitation".) And if we so choose, we may wish to explore in a future incarnation what leads someone to act in a particular way by deciding to experience exactly that. Indeed, how are we to know whether, in a previous incarnation, we didn't choose to be someone just like the person who has hurt us in this one? What if we've decided to experience the flipside of that – what it's like to be on the receiving end – as part of our growth?

"What have you learned and how have you grown in this lifetime, tender soul? Embrace it."

Challenging thoughts, for sure. But all the research suggests that we never go back to be met by judgement, but by healing and help to recover and understand. It certainly doesn't mean that someone who has behaved abusively doesn't feel shocked and horrified, doesn't feel remorse at what they've discovered they were capable of doing whilst immersed in the illusion of being human. And it doesn't mean that, when we sit down and go over the past life we've shared in our Soul Family, there isn't lots to explore and resolve. But the emphasis is on what we've learned and how we've grown. On restoration, not retribution. On healing.

HOW DO WE PREPARE FOR THE JOURNEY HOME?

What does all this mean for us, as we consider the start of the journey that's going to take a lifetime? It's helpful to continue with the analogy of a movie, just for now. It's as near perfect a parallel, in its process and execution, as I can think of, with which to create a working paradigm that will help us to conceptualize the tasks and stages involved in preparing for incarnation.

Prior to a movie reaching the cinema audience, a complex process has to take place to produce a viable production:

- There must be the desire to create, and a willingness to come together to do so.
- There has to be – in a good movie – a problem or predicament that will be worked out in the course of the movie.
- There has to be a storyline, with significant plot twists.
- Key characters need to be identified, each with a significant contribution to make to the success of the movie plot.
- In a memorable movie, those key characters often set out with obvious flaws, particular frailties and misperceptions, inaccurate beliefs or areas of misunderstanding.
- These are all laid out for the audience to see, while the characters are usually – at least initially – unaware of them.
- There are usually key characters (i.e. leading roles) and characters who contribute to the action by assisting or challenging them (i.e. through supporting roles).
- An effective plot involves a beginning, where the scene is set; a middle, where the main protagonist encounters major challenges, setbacks and plot twists – usually made more significant by their own personality traits or those flaws mentioned previously; and a satisfying ending, where necessary learning has been accomplished, helpful shifts have been made, and there has been a resolution of some kind.
- The ending isn't always a happy one for every character. While key characters have come through changed, others are clearly likely to continue in their old ways beyond the lifetime of the movie.

Alongside these basic needs of the storyline itself, suitable actors have to be assigned roles, and enter into a contract to play those roles within the movie. They agree to portray their character to the best of their ability, and to see it through right to the end. Each takes the time to understand their character's personality, their strengths and areas of weakness, their motives and the origin of the traits which underpin the choices they will make and the actions they will take in the movie. Crucially, a professional actor, committed to turning in an authentic performance, will do everything they can to make their identification with their character as complete as possible. Only then can they offer their fellow actors the experience required so that those actors, equally, can suspend disbelief for a time and enter into the illusion they are creating together.

"What part are you playing in the movie of your life, dear Child of the Universe?"

You'll notice that both plot and script, key protagonists and antagonists and all supporting roles are assigned, and the complex storyline agreed, before anyone begins to rehearse or film. Much of the preparation is carried out beforehand. By the time filming begins, the actors are quite a way along in the process of getting to know their characters and developing the empathy for them that is the cornerstone of any outstanding portrayal.

We might also usefully note that some roles, particularly those within major works of fiction or theatre, alongside remakes of much-loved films, are explored many times by different actors, each of whom bring their own unique perspective to their interpretation and portrayal of their chosen character within each new version.

So what has all this to do with us? How is it relevant to our own incarnation, our personal journey? What has a team of creative artists collaborating on a movie – which will hopefully influence and even change the lives of those who watch it and immerse themselves in the experiencing of it – got to do with us?

Well, this is precisely the sort of process that you and I, and every single human being on this planet, went through prior to being born in this lifetime. That's what all the research findings suggest. With great care, enormous consideration and detailed planning. Unless we are to discount a growing body of evidence gathered from people all over the planet, reporting similar experiences, describing the same processes and phenomena, the results of detailed, painstaking and meticulous research within reputable research institutions, then everything detailed above must inevitably apply to each one of us, too.

I have had many fascinating discussions over the years with those who have felt the need to resist such ideas. Often, those resisting have belonged to particular religious groups, and have been invested in preserving the teachings of their religion – at least, as we humans have interpreted them. Or they have convinced themselves that anything that science does not appear to be able to explain – by the way, I like to add the word "yet" here, and to ask which "science" the person is referring to – must be nonsense, wishful thinking or delusion. In terms of the assumption about wishful thinking, inherent in such comments, it's immensely helpful to read what author Dr Joe Dispenza has to say about the placebo effect in his book *You Are the Placebo,* and just how completely we have misunderstood it. The placebo effect – the power of a patient's belief in the medication they have received to heal them, even though it's in fact a placebo – actually corroborates the power of the mind.

"Resistance can show where we might be holding ourselves back, sweet soul. Always look for its gift."

It demonstrates that wishful thinking, supported by belief and intention, can affect the change the patient hopes for.

We must, of course, all be allowed the freedom to decide what we believe. We incarnate in order to go through a certain group of experiences, and this sometimes includes investing in particular beliefs and certain sets of rules. However, I have never met a truly evolved and spiritually enlightened soul that feared new ideas, new revelations. Such souls have inevitably reached a stage where curiosity has overtaken rigidity and fear. The fact that you were drawn to this book, and are reading it now, places you very firmly in that category. Hold your nerve!

In the next chapter, we're going to look at Soul Groups and the nature of Soul Contracts in more detail. And then consider your own story in the light of that. Right now, though, let's allow some space to take in all we've looked at in this one.

POCKET REFLECTION

Up until this point, you will have held certain beliefs about what has happened to you in this life so far. These are what have brought you to this point, where you are looking for a way to heal.

How do you feel about the possibility that healing might involve letting go of some of that? That it might mean learning to tell a different story, and hold a different set of perceptions about yourself and who you are? And about the other people in your story – both those who have been allies, and those who have seemed to be enemies? Or who have hurt you?

What does the story look like now? At this point? What feels the same? What has shifted a little?

What do you find yourself wanting to resist or fight? Why do you think that is? How might this be challenging you?

Amongst all the different people who have been part of your story, choose one – or two at most – who have helped or supported you. What have their gifts to you been?

Amongst all the different people who have been part of your story, choose one – or two at most – who have hurt you or let you down. What might their gifts to you have been?

Amongst all the different people who have been part of your story, choose one – two at most – who have presented you with choices, dilemmas. Maybe even brought about turning points. What might their gifts to you have been?

At this stage, just be curious. Even if your heart isn't particularly on board with this approach just now, give the practice a go anyway. What you choose to think or write in your Healing Journal matters less than the fact that you are thinking or writing.

I'm going to ask that you take lots of time at this point to digest what will have been, most likely, a great deal of different thinking. This point represents an important milestone. Everything you'll encounter from here on in will entail you being on board with the concepts that you've been invited to explore so far. So it's worth taking your time to allow yourself to stay here until you're ready to begin to look at your life, what happened before it, and the meaning and opportunities present in everything that has happened up to this point, from this new perspective.

This is your journey, sacred soul. No one is making you do this or putting any pressure on you in any way. All I'm offering is a way for you to heal. The best way I know how. It's how I finally healed – I'll share more of that later – and how I've help countless others to heal since. However, nothing is obligatory. You must be free at every step to do it in your own time and in your own way. You must be fully ready. Only you can judge when you feel that readiness happening. My role is simply to walk alongside you. You are doing everything perfectly, exactly as you came here to do.

CONNECT WITH YOUR SOUL SIGNATURE IN YOUR SACRED SPACE

Call to mind the word or phrase that you have imbued with the power of intention, and which always brings you to your Sacred Space. Speak it in your heart when you are ready. *Be here now.*

Take a little time to absorb the energy of this place. Slow your breathing, let all tension gradually drain away. Breathe in the peace and wellbeing of this place; let its stillness calm and soothe you.

Your heart will gradually beat to the one heartbeat. Become so present, so still, that you can feel that heartbeat. Your rhythm becomes the rhythm of the Universe. As you breathe in, you connect to all that is; as you breathe out, you let go, remembering that you are being breathed.

Take as much time as you need to become still. Remember the protective field that surrounds this Sacred Space. The outside world cannot enter here.

Take some time to feel in your body all that you are feeling. Anything that disturbs your peace. Don't push it away. That's not how healing happens. Compassion, acceptance, self-care is the way. The true medicine. There is space for everything that is coming up to be healed. Let it simply rest at the foot of the altar here. You don't need to do anything more.

In this Sacred Space there is always healing, a greater wisdom and knowing. It holds all you have forgotten; all you truly are. In here, you connect always with your eternal self, beyond time and space. The divinity that holds your humanity: your Soul Signature.

Let your Soul Signature show you a way to recognize its presence. All you need is already inside you. Just let it arise. Simply allow; don't try or force anything.

How does your Soul Signature make itself known to you right now? Through a sensation in your body? A vibration, a frequency? Don't rush this. You can't get it wrong. This is not a doing but a receiving. There's nothing you need to do. Your Soul Signature is already speaking to you.

Simply be here and focus on your breathing. Trust. Allow. Resist any temptation to decide that what you're sensing is imagination. Or wishful thinking. Or silly. Such concepts belong to time and space; they are part of the illusion. Part of forgetting. This is a Sacred Space. A portal to everything.

As you become aware of how your Soul Signature communicates with you, notice where you sense this in your body. Place your non-dominant hand there. Feel that sensation intensify. This is how you will connect. Anytime, anywhere. Whenever you need guidance, confirmation, place your hand here. Feel the sensation and allow.

This will be your way of instant connection. To this Sacred Space, to the infinite compassion and healing that is held here, to your true Higher Self beyond time and space. To your Soul Signature.

As you prepare to leave for now, take a final glance at the altar you created. Remind yourself of the significance of all you placed there. The longings, the hopes, the journey you have embarked upon. The path you are about to walk along.

Then place your non-dominant hand once again on that point of connection and feel your Soul Signature respond. You are safe and all is well.

Come back to the present. Decide what you need. Do that.

When you feel ready, share your thoughts and feelings with your Healing Journal.

Then take a break. Let it all sink in, settle. Take all the time you need.

POCKET TAKEAWAYS

Everything that exists is part of a vast field of intelligent, loving consciousness, which is constantly creating and evolving. A significant aspect of this evolution comes about through the process of incarnating and creating experiences in order to learn.

Within this field, we each exist as an individual energetic Essence (i.e. Soul Signature). Our soul is the part of the Essence that incarnates. Our Higher Self is the part that does not incarnate but which offers guidance and knows our life path and purpose. We sometimes call this our "inner voice" or "inner being".

We incarnate willingly and intentionally so as to encounter certain chosen experiences. To achieve this, we adopt a set of characteristics, and agree a particular set of circumstances and key life events that will help create the necessary backdrop for this encounter to happen.

Life between lives is loving, nurturing and restorative. We recognize, and are reunited with, our Soul Family and our guides. We are also helped to review, process and integrate the experiences and learning arising out of having incarnated.

It is entirely our choice whether or not to incarnate. If we do so, our decision arises out of a desire to grow or to help create an experience through which a fellow soul can grow too.

WHEN YOU HAVE FORGOTTEN...

We once believed that life was random, love was brief, and that death was final. It made everything feel precarious, bleak, without meaning or purpose.

WHEN YOU REMEMBER...

Now you hold a new truth: that life and love are forever, that nothing is ever lost. Knowing this brings profound peace.

3

THE POINT OF PAIN

Trauma: the event or experience that creates the wounds and themes we come to work through and heal.

"You came for this, tender soul. Everything you need is deep inside you. Available to you at all times."

So our life between lives is almost over … It's about to get serious. Not that life between lives isn't serious; rather, life between lives has a different quality. Subjects remembering the moment of leaving the body and returning home experience enormous relief, overwhelming emotion. There is joy and tears as they recognize familiar faces and places. It is an environment of kindness, acceptance. Serenity. The brutality that can be life on Earth has been survived; its beauty can be celebrated, the learning honoured. Now there is healing, rest, recuperation.

There is also concern for the grief and pain of those loved ones temporarily left behind. Frequently, the person who has just passed attempts to communicate that all is well. That they are still here, simply in an altered dimension. And that they will come and go at will, and certainly when called upon. Nevertheless, the human experience is over, they have survived and invariably managed the challenges they chose to face better than they believed they did. And they are met by a loving guide who has accompanied them through many lifetimes, together with Soul Family members with whom they enjoy a tearful and joyful reunion.

Here we are, however, about to consider the start of that adventure. And that involves looking at the Point of Pain (which is an event or more protracted experience) and the point of pain (that is, its purpose and central place in this human journey).

From our current viewpoint, in the thick of it all, the last thing we may be able to accept is that we might have chosen the experiences we've gone through. Are still going through. Are reeling from, desperate for it all to stop. In the middle of the experience of forgetting and the total amnesia that descends, the very last concept we're ready to take on board is that – as we see it from this perspective – somehow we did this to ourselves. Agreed it was okay. This pain. That there's some point to. Said, "Bring it on!" For many, this becomes a real sticking point. Understandably. At least, temporarily. Until the freedom from pain it offers begins to sink in and be felt.

A DIFFERENT PERSPECTIVE

How would we not feel this way? What a bitter pill to be asked to swallow! If that's your reaction right now, that's absolutely fine. Completely understandable. Suffering is bad enough, without the added insult of being told that we chose for it to happen! What New Age rubbish is this! What a neat way of trying to legitimize the outrageous, the unacceptable. The unforgivable.

However, we're going to give this a bit more thought. Because telling our self these things, seeing it this way, creates and perpetuates enormous pain. It turns us into a helpless victim. It means that life is random. It means the Universe is cruel or indifferent. It means that there is no help, no guidance, no support. It makes us a pawn in a game that something or someone else is playing. Back to our early discussions: it leaves us running scared.

So while it can seem comforting to blame others, and to buy in to the story that we have been wronged, it creates lifelong suffering. Woundedness. Bitterness. Fear and anxiety about our inability to survive whatever might happen next.

Let's share all this in your journal. Work things out a bit. Consider possibilities. Some turnarounds.

POCKET REFLECTION

Take some time to allow whatever you're feeling at this point to surface. All the different feelings.

Check the sensations going on in your body. Where are they? What message do they have for you?

How does it feel to be moving on to this next chapter? With its difficult title? And the anticipation of what's to come?

Maybe there's fear? An anxiety of not knowing?

Are you going to be asked to revisit difficult places? Distant memories that feel not that distant at all?

Am I going to ask you to let go of parts of your story you still feel invested in? That you don't want to give up yet? Am I trying to persuade you to believe that pain is somehow a necessary experience? Something we must go through?

And what about that idea – the inconceivable hypothesis – that we plan and intend it, this pain?

Alongside all of this, however, there might be a flickering of something else? Something more liberating? That if such a different way of looking at things exists, then perhaps it might hold some wisdom, some truth that can help? Since other possibilities don't seem to have shifted anything much? Or brought lasting relief? Or permanent change? That we might together manage to end this? That it can finally be over?

Be with all of this awhile. Then, when you're ready, come and join me.

So let's think this through. Carefully. In the light of all we've considered so far. Let's honour those feelings, cradle them close and rock them gently. Soothe them down a little. Let's sit together a while, open our bag of provisions, get out the map. Let's look at the journey so far, reminding ourselves that this is all about healing. About perception and perspective. About suspending old beliefs for a time because they haven't served us and haven't brought the peace we crave, the understanding we long for.

WHY "THE POINT OF PAIN"?

I chose the title of this stage of the journey with great care. I called it many things before settling on "The Point of Pain". I tried words such as "trauma" in an attempt to give it its full impact and appropriate weight; I swung the other way, to words such as "contrast" and "challenge" in an attempt to do the opposite and soften the blow. In the end, I realized I needed to question why I was avoiding what was real: pain. "Trauma" describes one of the major effects of pain, but not its complete nature; "contrast" attempts to deny its full impact by rationalizing it away. "Challenges" downplays it to the point of insult.

We have such a tendency to want to sanitize the messy. To pathologize the open wound and stitch it up before anyone sees it. Or medicate it away because any state that's not happiness is to be eradicated. Just as the Victorians covered the legs of tables because for them there could be no hint of anything that might have sexual overtones, yet they could face death and honour grieving, we have done something similar through our ability to begin to embrace sexuality and gender identity, while needing to deny the existence of pain. Appropriate pain. Inevitable pain. We have become pain averse. And in so doing, we have done a great disservice to the process which, above all others, leads us to grow and transform. And which, as research into the process of spiritual awakening – or, as I might call it, "remembering" – clearly demonstrates, is one of the prime movers in triggering the awakening process.

There is a growing body of thinking by those whose original area of expertise has been in the understanding of trauma and new ways of releasing it – renowned figures such as Bessell Van der Kolk, author of *The Body Keeps The Score*, and Peter Levine, renowned for his ground-breaking works *In an Unspoken Voice*, *Trauma Through a Child's Eyes* and *Waking The Tiger* – which is now recognizing and incorporating a further stage that reveals itself in the healing of trauma: that of awe.

Such research now concludes that the experience of awe – arising from our recognition that we have survived something we believed we couldn't survive – is a key component that arises out of the healing of trauma. And that this having survived is true of everyone we see. This recognition leads us to access parts of a deeper self within us, which we might call our Soul Signature. This, in turn, gives rise to a process which, through the intersection between certain mystical energy systems and our own nervous system, appears to open the way to our appreciation of Oneness and non-duality.

Can you let that thought in? Can you begin to see how heroic simply surviving is? And what it reveals about you that you may not even have appreciated?

While pain is invariably unwelcome while we're going through it, when we look back, having come out the other side, we usually recognize its gift. We appreciate that, because of experiencing it, having survived it and been changed by it, certain things have happened that wouldn't otherwise have taken place.

Let's look at what we know about pain and its effects:

- It challenges us to dig deep and find qualities inside us we didn't know were there.
- It brings a new perspective: our sense of our priorities or what we count as important or less important shifts.
- We are changed by the commonality we now share with others, which expands our empathy and understanding of being One with all others on the planet.

- We discover truths about ourselves we wouldn't otherwise have discovered – positive and negative – and grow in self-knowledge and awareness.
- Our pain has been transformative, in that we are forever changed by the experience.
- It encourages a sense of awe and non-duality.
- It offers the possibility of spiritual growth, wisdom and spiritual awakening.

While pain achieves these things, its opposites – relief, joy, peace – help us to recover from the experience of pain, to process it, to feel safe again and restored. And to use it as a catalyst for growth, appreciation, gratitude. This tends to happen in hindsight, after the painful event. But it can also happen during brief lulls or moments of intense connection or beauty within the experience of pain itself.

Even in the initial stages of planning and thinking about the nature of this book, as I tried to position it, and work out what it would offer that might be different, there was some concern that people really might not want to read a book about pain. But that's precisely the point: we tread on eggshells around pain because we dread it, it appears to be overwhelmingly negative. Wouldn't the world be better off if we could eradicate it?

Well, have you ever met a human being who hasn't been touched and changed by pain? If we could find such a person, who would we encounter? I would suggest this person would appear unaware, lacking in empathy or sensitivity, unmoved by the plight of others, likely to be self-centred and lacking in an appreciation for the differing experiences of others. I would suggest that this, in its own right – were such a person to exist – would in fact involve a different kind of pain, since that person's ability to relate and experience satisfying relationships would be likely to be severely compromised.

Now compare that to your experience of someone who has known pain, and who has worked through that pain to a place of acceptance, integration, wisdom and gratitude. The genuinely great souls have all been transformed by experiencing pain and moving through it. In every one of these souls, you will see the awe mentioned above.

TRUE BRAVERY

So let's revisit pain. Let's champion it instead of dreading or fearing it. Pain is that inescapable human experience which, as spiritual beings come for an authentic experience of what it is to be human, is the central element for which we incarnate. Not in any masochistic way – which is how we might interpret such a desire from our current state of forgetting – but to deepen our compassion and capacity for empathy and understanding. Our appreciation of Oneness. The growing and expanding of all that is. Here you are, reading this, seeking your truth, sensing there's more and looking for answers beyond the obvious, because you have known pain. As has every fellow soul on this planet. No one is immune. And that makes us brave. Brave beyond our comprehension.

This chapter is going to focus on two truths at the centre of the healing journey. The first is that there is a Point of Pain – a point in time when we experience pain of such a specific quality that we might call it trauma and spend the rest of our lives trying to resolve it. This point of pain normally, though not in every case, happens during the early years of our life on this Earth. While we might remember later or subsequent points of pain, these are often repeats or mirrors of that original Point of Pain which trigger the original pain all over again.

The second is that there is a point to pain. That is, the point of pain is to achieve something specific. To bring something about. That point of pain acts as a catalyst for everything that follows. It instigates the learning journey – and the nature of the healing journey – that we will spend a lifetime exploring. If you like, it guides and directs both our Soul Path (the learning journey) and our Soul Purpose (the healing journey). And yes, they are different. Our Soul Purpose is to awaken and grow, become even more; our Soul Path is the human experience we have chosen to go through in order to achieve that awakening and growth.

POCKET REFLECTION

Take some time now to review your story. Your pain.

Instead of focussing on what it felt like and/or feels like now, see if instead you can find and appreciate how it has stretched you, grown you.

Allow yourself to take in the truth that you have survived. Not by accident, or some fluke of fate. But through your own strength and resilience. Your own resourcefulness and creativity. Through finding ways to get through. Don't judge how; focus on the truth that you found a way.

Can you see this as the act of bravery it truly is?

If you had witnessed someone else going through what you have gone through, and finding ways to hold on, to get through, what would you say to them?

Can you say that to yourself? Do that now, in your Healing Journal.

THE CENTRALITY OF TRAUMA

Essentially, our Point of Pain is the experience that creates trauma memory. And trauma memory is what we spend a lifetime trying to resolve, heal and move beyond into freedom. It's what we experience every time we are triggered: our Point of Pain is how the original trigger of our suffering comes into being.

Much that is written on trauma, and most studies carried out, have quite rightly focussed upon what we tend to think of as the severe end of the trauma spectrum. This has meant that, when I use the word "trauma" to describe what a client has experienced, they will frequently push it back, saying that what they have experienced isn't bad enough to be called that. So at this point I'm going to explain what trauma is at its core – and why there isn't a human being on this Earth who hasn't experienced it ...

Trauma is the complex response – involving the body, the brain and the energy system – to any situation in which we didn't feel safe, and where it has been felt there was either inadequate help, indifference, or no help at all. Studies by Babette Rothschild, author of *The Body Remembers*, and Peter Levine, author of *In an Unspoken Voice*, in particular, have normalized and elaborated upon this central element. However, for the purpose of this journey we're making together, we're going to add an additional dimension. I would suggest that underlying all trauma – the sense of fear and threat, and the feeling of being alone without help, there being no witness and no support – is the experience of forgetting. And the subsequent belief that we are separate. In this on our own.

Traumatic memory is held in our nervous system and in our energy body, and its release can be dramatic.

GEORGIE'S STORY

I recall a client – let's call her Georgie – who came for energy healing for help with always feeling tired and tense. We talked in depth before the healing session, identifying how much fear Georgie had experienced growing up amongst a group of warring siblings, all brothers, and how she had never felt safe because her parents never intervened. As Georgie lay on my reiki table and the energy began to flow, her body began to shake uncontrollably. I asked if she wanted us to stop, but she told me she could feel something massive, like a heavy rock in her chest, disintegrating and she wanted to continue.

The shaking intensified, as I focussed my attention on her chest and solar plexus. Then came the tears. Years and years of fear, shame at being afraid, and then the anger at feeling helpless. Unsafe. Gradually the shaking calmed, to be replaced by a sense of overwhelming calm and wellbeing. Georgie described it as feeling bathed in sunlight.

And following this, Georgie found her voice. For the first time, she was able to speak feelings she had believed she had to hold in for fear of upsetting others. Through our work together, Georgie found a way to initiate healing conversations with her parents and her brothers and to change a childhood dynamic into an adult one. That is, to replace the silence that comes with the freeze response with the empowerment that comes from release. We'll talk more about different responses to trauma in chapter 4.

THE HIDDEN NATURE OF TRAUMA

It feels important to say that not all trauma is obvious. Some clients who come to see me know at the outset what they are trying to heal; others do not. They simply know that all is not well. Maybe they can't free themselves of chronic worry;

perhaps they find they're unable to make a relationship last. Often, it's a generalized sense that they are not happy. That they don't even know what happiness looks or feels like. Can't still a busy mind or find peace. Always, as we begin to explore further, there is a Point of Pain.

It's also helpful to emphasize that there isn't always – in fact, rarely is there – a single definable point of pain. A discrete moment in time. More often, our Point of Pain is created by a repeating experience – a "drip, drip" rather than a tidal wave. It is usually, though not always, those souls who incarnate to take the role of a parent who journey with us to give us those experiences necessary for our Soul Path. Josh's experience is a typical example, as we'll see.

JOSH'S STORY

Josh had grown up with a father who frequently lost his temper. His father was stressed and anxious about life in general, and his outbursts were unpredictable. Josh never knew when his father might explode at him. On a good day – maybe on holiday, when the demands of life were a bit fewer – his father could be fun and laugh and play with him; on a bad day, what had one day been acceptable and fun would suddenly result in rage and punishment.

Josh described how, one swelteringly hot day, his father connected up a hose pipe, attached a spray nozzle, and played a game with him in which they both got soaked, laughing and splashing and aiming the nozzle at each other. His voice cracking, Josh then explained how the following night, after his father got home from work, Josh had hidden in the garden waiting for his dad to come and look at the flower beds as he always did. Then he had turned on the hose and sprayed it at his father exactly like they had done in the game the previous day.

His father was livid. He grappled the hose out of Josh's hands, tore it off the tap – breaking the tap connector in the process – and flung it in the dustbin. He then shouted at Josh to go to his room and think about what a bad boy he had been, saying there would be no more games if that was how they made him behave.

By the time Josh came to see me, at a loss as to how to deal with a female line manager at work who could easily "fly off the handle at nothing", he was able to describe, with my encouragement, a whole series of similar encounters throughout his life. Initially, those incidents had appeared unconnected, a series of random encounters all of which proved challenging. Each time, he would become scared and anxious, believing it was his fault, and that he needed to learn to be more sensitive and careful.

As we looked more deeply into the actual healing Josh had come to do, we were able to identify a number of life themes, all going back to his Point of Pain. And that was? A relationship with his father which was never safe or satisfying, in which Josh felt he always got it wrong. And Josh's subsequent mistrust of intimacy and closeness, and his absolute belief that his love was inevitably damaging to the other person. This was trauma.

MARIAM'S STORY

Mariam's story is another typical example of trauma. Mariam came to see me for help to understand how, every time she got into a serious relationship, she would become needy and insecure, possessive and punishing. Again, this had become an identifiable pattern in her life. She was appalled at the way in which she "turned into some kind of monster" when, normally, she believed herself to be a well-balanced and independent woman.

She told me how she had witnessed, as a little girl, fights between her parents which frequently culminated in her mother packing her suitcase and leaving home. She could recall being given no explanation for them and no promise that her mother would return. One time, her mother stayed away for several weeks, during which time she had no contact with Mariam. This was trauma.

JEROME'S STORY

Some trauma is so every day we can easily miss that it's trauma at all. Jerome's mother was an anxious woman, a worrier. If ever Jerome seemed unhappy, she would be desperate for him to be happy again. If he was worried about something, hurt or upset, she would tell him that knowing about it had meant she was unable to sleep. As Jerome got older, he learned that it wasn't possible to share anything other than positive bits of news or achievements with her, because her reactions to anything else left him feeling guilty and selfish. This was trauma.

MELISSA'S STORY

Sometimes what we think of as being the obvious source of our pain isn't at all. Melissa's dad suffered with bipolar disorder. He would have immense highs, during which he was fun and exciting, although quick to anger if she ever told him that his ideas/his suggestions for adventures sometimes made her scared or were unrealistic. He would also experience terrible lows, during which he would take little or no interest in her, say cruel things, drink heavily and at times speak of ending his life. Consequently, Melissa learned to tread on eggshells around him, and protect her heart, which was inevitably going to be broken each time he became severely depressed. So for Melissa, it wasn't the drinking, the anger, the threats to kill himself that were the source of the trauma, though these were certainly traumatizing. Melissa's actual point of pain was that she came to believe that no one could love her consistently, or that she was sufficiently worthy of love that someone would be willingly to hang around. This was trauma.

MANY FAMILIES, ONE SOUL FAMILY

Incidentally, before any of us move toward any kind of judgement here – criticizing parents and those who seem inadequate as parents, or their choices – do you know one of the most moving things that I came across in my research into life between lives? It came from people who recalled their soul entering the body of the unborn child they were to become, and who remembered how they had practised – prior to incarnating – ways to soothe the mother during labour and childbirth. I found so many recollections recorded of the baby's concern for the mother, their soul radiating love and calm, trying to reach through to her and communicate energetically with her. Indeed, some people under hypnosis – especially children – recall practising how to do this prior to their soul entering the foetus. And this, as we are coming to understand, despite everything that is to come, including whatever pain, failures to love or lack of understanding that have been planned in advance.

Are you beginning to see just how far this unconditional acceptance goes? The depth of love that is Oneness?

As research into life between lives demonstrates, we have all offered each other, within our Soul Group or Soul Family, many alternative experiences. We have adopted different gender roles and identities, and explored sexuality, disability, culture, race, class, good, evil and everything in between. We have been both the victim and the perpetrator. One of the interesting findings to come out of research documented in Richard Martini's book *Flipside*, and studies into previous lives such as those examined by Michael Newton in *Journey of Souls*, relates to individuals who recalled the Holocaust under hypnosis.

It emerged, through many recollections under hypnosis, that those who had suffered at the hands of their perpetrators invariably felt enormous compassion for them. This was for two reasons: firstly, a perpetrator must be formed out of early experiences that lead to a propensity for cruelty and inhumanity; secondly, the perpetrator's remorse after death – and prior to the reorientation which comes from remembering that everything had been agreed – is initially considerable, and the need for rest and recovery great.

As I read this research, my mind went back to my partner's mother, communicating with me in the hospital corridor as her body lay close to death. Telling me that being the kind of mother she had been had presented her with one of her most painful challenges.

It's so hard, isn't it, to get our heads around this – let alone our hearts – when we're in the thick of forgetting? We feel indignation. Outrage. I myself have had many a furious exchange in the past with anyone who held that this could be so. In the midst of duality, concepts such as "victim" and "perpetrator" feel so real. We throw ourselves into stories of good guys and bad guys, we split reality into boxes and categories, we preach and pronounce. And then, with an open mind, we start to explore other viewpoints, research that offers a starkly different perspective.

> "Let it be complicated, lovely one.
> Many viewpoints can be true
> at the same time."

Years ago, when I first came across Byron Katie's work and read *A Mind at Home with Itself* and *I Need Your Love*, I was horrified to hear her say that anyone could accuse her of anything, and she could find it to be true. Anything? What – does she mean murder? Torture? Abuse? Really? Now I understand that, once we understand Oneness and non-duality, what one knows, we all know; what one has experienced, we have all experienced; what one has done, we have all done.

And when one heals, we all heal. Remember?

POCKET REFLECTION

Take a moment to connect once more with your own story. Are there particular kinds of situations you seem to keep finding yourself in? Let yourself allow those into your awareness.

Go gently with yourself while you do this. Hold an attitude of kindness; be interested, as if you were watching a character in a movie. Stay back, watch at a distance. You are recalling trauma.

You're not here to judge, or to hold yourself or anyone else to account. You're simply observing and looking for a pattern.

Let any feelings that arise simply flow through you. If you accept them and don't try to prevent them, they will quickly die down.

Are there certain kinds of people that you find more challenging than others? More than usually difficult to manage or deal with? Do you see your own trauma here?

Are there types of behaviour you might encounter in someone that would lead you to behave in a way you're unhappy about? Or puzzled by? How does your own trauma play a part in this?

Are there things that particularly trigger you repeatedly, and which pull you into the same feelings and behaviours time after time?

How do you feel right now? Where are you? In the past or in the present?

> Take several gentle breaths in and then slow breaths out. Connect with your body. Notice the rise and fall in your chest. Your abdomen. Become aware that you are here now. Here and safe in this embracing stillness.

This is very probably one of the most challenging points in the journey we're making together. It's going to shake up a lot, looking at things in this different way. It will challenge a way of seeing that has caused so much suffering up to this point. However, in doing so, it's going to involve us letting go of some dearly held beliefs. I don't begin to pretend this is easy. It's one of the hardest things you'll ever be asked to do on this journey of healing.

The way you've told the story of your lifetime will no longer work once we switch this torch on. I want you to know how profoundly I understand what a huge task that can be. The depth of the emotion involved. The investment in the story that's served you so well up to now. The resistance. The tears of loss. The anger and resentment that somehow "they" are getting away with it.

As always, take as much time as you need. There are no "shoulds" or "oughts" here. There's just you. And me. And a journey of healing. And an entire Universe of guides, healers and helpers, so many who have always known and loved you looking on. Nothing changes how much you are regarded with gratitude and awe, and appreciated, and unconditionally accepted. There's nothing you can do wrong. You can't make a mistake here. Love holds you. Lean in.

TELLING A DIFFERENT STORY

While you're doing that, I'd like to share with you my own Point of Pain. I think it might help. When you read it, don't be tempted to create some sort of hierarchy of pain – something we humans love to do: "My pain is greater than yours, so how can you possibly understand?" or, "Your pain is greater than mine so how can I possibly think mine is worthy of being called pain?" Read it from the perspective of Oneness: everything you've known, and everything I've known, we've all known.

I'm going to tell you about my Point of Pain in a particular way, one that will hopefully illustrate in some small sense how this all works. So here goes. See what you think …

MY STORY

Among the key members of my Soul Family who agreed to incarnate with me, and to provide me with the Point of Pain that I would spend a significant part of this lifetime being challenged by, and trying to resolve, were the souls who would take the role of my mother, my father, my stepmother, my paternal grandmother and my maternal grandmother. These were the key players. Other souls have become more prominent since, but they are not relevant here. Other souls also played smaller parts in the original drama, but for the sake of simplicity and clarity I won't include them here.

The key events that created the Point of Pain for the soul who incarnated as Janny are these:

- Janny was a greatly anticipated and much-loved baby.
- Five days after Janny was born, her mother dropped dead in the hospital corridor from a sudden pulmonary embolism.
- Janny's father was distraught and wanted nothing to do with the baby, without whose birth his wife would not have died.
- Janny's paternal grandmother and grandfather moved in with her father to look after the little girl.

- In that naïve way that children have, Janny believed her grandmother to be her mother and formed a deep attachment to her, and she to her.
- Janny's father gradually began to accept and take an interest in her, but she always had the sense – nothing was ever said – that she had done something awful and that her mere presence caused him great pain.
- Janny's father remarried when she was three years old.
- Without Janny knowing why, her grandmother suddenly moved out with her grandfather. Janny couldn't understand what she had done to make her grandmother go, and why she no longer wanted to be her mother.
- Janny's grandmother and grandfather moved into a farm cottage (Janny remained in the main farmhouse) about a hundred yards up the road, where from her bedroom window Janny could still see her grandmother hanging out the washing, but could no longer reach her.
- The second marriage was problematic and unhappy. Janny's stepmother was a tortured woman, who felt unlovable and resented other people's happiness.
- She was jealous of Janny's father's evident continuing love for Janny's mother, of Janny for being the product of that union, and of her grandmother for being the one that Janny loved and pined for. Consequently, her stepmother would mock that love, try to make Janny feel like it was wrong, and made it difficult for her to visit her grandmother without feeling guilty and disloyal.
- Janny's father was torn, feeling increasingly unable to show his daughter affection in the house because it would cause an argument, and only seeming able to do so in secret when they were out on the farm together.
- When arguments over the situation became particularly heated, Janny's father would ask her stepmother if she would prefer Janny to go and live with her grandmother.

- At such times, it seemed to Janny as if he held the power to bring relief and was holding out a promise, a possibility.
- Every time, her stepmother would initially say yes, but then fear of shame and failure would make her retract.
- Janny could never understand why he wouldn't let her go.
- She could also never understand why her grandmother didn't love her enough to come and rescue her from the situation.
- Janny's maternal grandmother was unable to recover from the loss of Janny's mother.
- Since she lived a distance away, Janny would be taken to spend a week at a time with her. During this time, she could not let Janny out of her sight, endlessly reminiscing, seeing elements of her daughter in her granddaughter, and reliving her grief through her.
- So, for Janny, love came to mean either the pain of not being loved in return, or being suffocated and smothered by another's need of her.

So here, then, you have my Point of Pain. The Point of Pain that the soul that is me came to experience in this lifetime. The pain is no longer raw, and I've done a great deal of work on that story, what it left me with, what it challenged me to go through and overcome, the learning that came from it, and the consequences of it in terms of the path my life has taken and where it has brought me to at this current time. There have been many other painful experiences, along with numerous joyful and beautiful ones along the way.

However, pain teaches melancholy, which is a prerequisite for kindness and compassion, which, in its turn, is necessary for spiritual awakening. And here I find myself, sitting at my laptop, writing this. Directly for you. With your healing uppermost in my mind. Sharing this journey with you. As I believe I was always meant to do.

So that's me. And my point of pain and consequent journey. My task has been to do exactly what I'm here to keep you company in doing: to embrace the total experience, in Oneness. To see the challenges I chose, and where they have taken me. To feel gratitude – yes, I do feel gratitude – toward every single player in my drama. Which I can now appreciate to be the movie it always was.

In that drama, this movie, every single player made enormous sacrifices in coming to experience dramas of their own, which were themselves excruciatingly painful, and which led to their having to resolve challenges in their own journeys.

A MESSAGE FROM BEHIND THE BARRIER

Some years ago, my partner became aware of the presence of a woman, who kept trying to make herself known. My partner has had the ability, since childhood, to see and hear those who have passed on. As a child this terrified her, but more recently she had become less afraid and more open to the possibility that sometimes she could be of service by allowing herself to act as an intermediary.

The woman in question was persistent to the point of becoming irritating. She appeared as a young woman, talking animatedly and so fast and furiously that trying to make out what she was saying was frustratingly difficult. My partner said she knew it was my mother, but that she was behaving like a screaming teenager might in the heady days of the Beatles. She mimicked to me what she heard and saw: this woman holding her hands to her face and screaming madly as if standing behind a barrier, watching the Beatles arrive, desperate to be let through so she could run to them, yet unable to do so. It seemed crazy and made no sense. Why would my mother show herself like this? What was she trying to convey?

Then, one weekend, we decided to give her some focussed space. I sat quietly as my partner grounded herself and allowed my mother to communicate with her. My partner had just begun to settle into this when my mother's energy suddenly merged with her own and my mother was finally able to show us what she had been trying to say.

It wasn't the Beatles at all. And it wasn't a physical barrier holding back crowds of screaming fans. My partner described, with tears of grief, shock, and disbelief, my mother's felt experience in the actual moment of finding herself parted from her baby as her soul left her body and she realized that she was separated. The screaming had been for the loss of her baby, and the sense of a barrier was the arms around her ready to help her understand what had happened. Once my mother had shown us this, the emotion calmed, to be replaced by a stillness, as she told Nicky how desperately she had fought in that moment to stay, and her sense of utter helplessness at not being able to protect her baby or keep her safe. Because we are fractals of energy, we can convey parts of an experience in this way, and communicate a message to a loved one, even as the greater portion of the energy we are continues its existence elsewhere. It is a psychic communication only.

She wanted to me to know that she was always nearby. Always aware. It was an amazingly simple message.

But what it achieved was profound. I was suddenly able to welcome in the knowledge that she had loved me, to replace what had felt to be simply an absence. A lack. So often, clients will describe their trauma as being a "void". This is particularly the case for those whose trauma stems from feeling invisible, not having been seen. And underneath this, or within it, is the existential terror of psychic aloneness. Of being separate and isolated. It is the absolute antithesis of the experience of Oneness.

THE TWO FUNDAMENTAL SOURCES OF TRAUMA

I have found that our knowledge of trauma often stems from one of two possible, apparently opposing, experiences: those that involve abandonment, and those that involve intrusion. Abandonment is not always physical – we can emotionally or psychologically abandon a child without ever actually going away; similarly, while we might immediately think of intrusion as being to do with sexual or physical abuse, which is, of course, one significant and devastating type of invasion, it can also take the form of giving a child no psychic space or peace, wanting to know everything they think or do, and trying to dominate or control them. It can also – and frequently does – take the form of the projection by a parent of their feelings into a child. The child then becomes a container for the parent's feelings, often later in life describing themselves as having had to be a parent while their actual parent was like a child.

Trauma – this Point of Pain which is a universal experience in this human journey – is everywhere we look. As well as individual trauma, there is family trauma, generational and intergenerational trauma, trauma at the level of cultures and peoples, societies and global trauma. Planet Earth is not an easy place to incarnate. It offers the toughest challenges and the greatest opportunities for growth, evolving wisdom and expansion in compassion. Only the bravest souls, and the most generous, the most highly evolved, come for this. And because you are here, this must be true of you. Or you would not, could not, be here. Now.

Pain is everywhere. Hurt is everywhere. Trauma is universal. As are love and beauty, forgiveness and healing. And it is in this sense, because we are one consciousness, one unified field of love and compassion endlessly expanding, that I offer the only way out I know. For when one heals, we all heal.

"Pain is universal. We have all known hurt. Hurt people hurt people. Only compassion can heal this."

Where are you right now, gentle soul, on this momentous journey? How is it with you? As we sit here together, having taken a bit of a breather while I shared some of my own journey, are you ready yet to continue with your own?

If so, we're going to put some of what we've discovered to the hardest test of all: beginning to apply it to our own life.

TWO CHOICES

As we do this, I'm really offering you a choice. You can stick to the story you have built so far – the one you would tell friends, or the background you might give to your therapist. No one is going to ask you to give that up. You don't have to say those things that have happened to you didn't happen, or that they didn't cause you enormous pain and suffering. At no point will I be asking you to deny any of that or diminish those experiences in any way. You won't ever be asked to say none of it mattered.

On the contrary, we're going to do the exact opposite. We're going to give your story the gravity and weight it deserves. We're going to validate and honour every single part of it. But we're going to do this – if you're willing – from a far bigger perspective. A cosmic one, not an individual one. It doesn't lessen the impact or importance of your story in any way. But it does make it less personal. And less personal is always less painful.

The choice I'm going to offer you is this:

1. You can continue, if you so wish, to tell your story in a human way, from the perspective of someone so immersed in this time–space reality that this is all there is. In this

version, you will be a victim of circumstance, in a world where cruel things happen randomly to good people, unfairly and without consequence. You will place yourself at the centre of this story, rather than at the centre of the cosmos. And your one life will have no greater significance than that you were here for a while, had some good times and some bad ones, affected those close to you, and were affected by a few others.

2. Or you can allow your life to have a far greater significance. This means seeing it from the perspective of Oneness, to become far bigger. To become complete. In this second version of your story, everything that has happened has had profound and lasting meaning. Nothing has been accidental, since at no point have you been separate from the cosmic flow within which you exist.
In this version, therefore, your one life – and all that has happened in it – has reverberated through eternity, and for all eternity. It is impossible for that not to be so, since it is forever held within the energy that comprises all that is. Nothing is lost; nothing has been pointless or irrelevant. It is forever part of the fabric of the Universe itself.

While you're taking some time to consider, I want to tell you about an experience that one of my clients had recently. We can call her Gemma.

A PURPLE DRAGON

Gemma had come to see me to explore her inner child. She wanted to do some visualization and some journeying. So we set out together, using a steady drumbeat to aid her in that search. She found herself walking through a forest, then out into different terrain, rockier and more barren, where she noticed a tower on the top of a hill. Approaching it, she saw that the tower was sparkling and shimmering. And on entering, she saw that there was a circular staircase going upwards from the ground level, the floor of which was made of bare rock.

As Gemma climbed higher – the stairs seemed to go on and on – she had a gathering certainty that the inner child she had come to meet was inside the top of the tower. She felt nervous, not sure what she was going to find. In her mind's eye, she saw a child in a ragged dress slumped against the wall, sobbing. She dreaded the effect that this was going to have on her. So much so that she almost decided to turn around and descend the stairs without entering the room. Nevertheless she held her nerve, and went in.

What met her was astonishing, and totally unexpected. Far from seeing a helpless, broken little girl curled up in a ball, she was met by a purple dragon. The dragon was playful, nimble, friendly and full of laughter and mischief. Completely irrepressible. Jumping here, bouncing there. Brimming with enthusiasm and excitement. The dragon invited Gemma to jump on its back, and they flew off together through the turret window.

"Our inner child is never wounded. It is gloriously free, waiting to free *us*."

We so often misunderstand our inner child. We spend so much time trying to address the part of us that we believe is our inner child, telling them how much they are safe, loved, and worthy, not realizing that the part we're speaking to is our wounded, traumatized part. The part of the personality that has been hurt and seemingly damaged by its early human experience. Our true "inner child" is not this at all. It is untouched by human trauma because it is pristine and divine. It isn't the sobbing child crumpled on the floor; it is the ebullient, confident purple dragon. The part of us that is forever in touch with our Soul Signature, witnessing the adventure, but never immersed in it. And most definitely never overwhelmed by it.

So, are you ready? Shall we do this? You know what's coming; will you give it a go? Shall we take this next step on your own healing journey? Shall we change perspective?

POCKET REFLECTION

Have a think now about your own story. Just the beginnings. Find your own Point of Pain.

And write down everything in your Healing Journal in the third person, like you're sharing the plot line of a movie, rather than reliving it yourself. Exactly as I did in my account earlier, starting with: "The soul that in this lifetime is called … "

Don't go too close to your story. You don't have to relive it. You've done that once already. It's over. Done. You'll never have to do it again. Ever. All you now have to do is find your path to healing. That's why we're here. Hold that thought close.

So now, take some time. Tell the story of that Point of Pain exactly as I told mine. (If it helps, go back and see what I wrote.) Just the headlines. The bullet points. We're not reliving, we're reworking. We're looking on in awe.

And it's a movie. A choice. None of it is who you really are. None of it is real. Record it in your Healing Journal in that way.

When you've finished, give yourself recovery time. Tenderly, gently with all the love and care you would want to give to someone who had just been through what you've described.

You may need to sleep, or to shake it out: laugh, dance, get out in nature. You may need a hug. A conversation. A warm drink. To snuggle up with your pet. To have a bath. A shower. Listen to music. Shadow box. Beat a drum. Laugh at a comedy. Cry to a sad movie.

The Point of Pain is central to every single one of our stories. The story that sets us on our journey to heal. That offers us the choice: to remain in forgetting, or to begin to remember. To awaken. You have achieved something amazing today.

This is one of the most significant of your Journal entries so far, so honour it, and honour your lived experience.

It takes time, and patience and enormous compassion to begin to heal our wounded parts. The hurt can be so great that we keep it in the shadows, out of sight – though its echoes never cease to haunt us – for years. And then, when the time is right and we're ready, we find we can dare to look it in the eyes. Finally. And when we do, we see that it has simply been waiting, all this time, to be welcomed in, be met with kindness and understanding, and to be helped to heal.

Rest and Heal in Your Sacred Space

Using your word or phrase of intention, bring yourself to your Sacred Space. *Be here now.*

As you enter, feel how soothing the energy is here. Today you have come here to be restored. What do you need? What is coming up for healing?

Listen to your heart. Let your Soul Signature guide you. The entire Universe knows what just happened, and you are loved and held.

There is wisdom here, answers. And in this space, there is nothing but awe and admiration for you.

You become aware of how weary you are; how burdened you have been feeling. You sense an invitation to lie down. You look around for a suitable place. As you choose it, everything transforms for your comfort. The surrounding light dims, and you lie down upon the softest surface. You sink down into it, surrounded by scented candles, relaxing sounds – soft music, or Earth songs. Somewhere water trickles from a fountain or waterfall.

Figures emerge from the dimness. You feel no alarm – their energy is loving, kind. You understand that they are here to restore your strength.

It seems the most natural occurrence; it's as if you've known this before. These figures have the most beautiful eyes; you could lose yourself in the depth of understanding they hold. You find that, as you meet their gaze, all your pain dissolves.

You don't know how, but you realize these figures have always known you; have tended to you like this before. You feel a cool hand on your forehead, a fizzing warmth spread through your entire being. Until this is all there is. Healing, cleansing.

You feel something break open inside you. Something that had been hard, rigid, is now softening. It is being bathed by this warm energy flowing into you; through you. Then somewhere else, something gives way. A pain you didn't even realize was there is easing, settling.

You notice that if you focus on a particular incident, person, or memory, you can now detect where it is lodged in your body. And that you can direct this flow of energy toward it. That this energy can dissolve or transform it. Effortlessly. You close your eyes and practise this new skill. It feels such a joyous relief.

When you open your eyes, all is as it once was. The light has returned to normal; the figures have disappeared.

But they have left something with you. It's there in your hands. A reminder, a symbol.

You examine this gift, pondering its meaning until you know it. Then you walk over to the altar and place it there.

As you come back, allow yourself to take this truth, this message, deep into your being.

When you feel ready, share your thoughts and feelings with your Healing Journal.

POCKET TAKEAWAYS

- Trauma is not limited to certain individuals. Everyone comes to experience – and overcome – their own Point of Pain.
- Our Point of Pain propels us fully into the illusion that we are in an unsafe world.
- It is the experience that sets us on the path of healing and growth.
- Our individual Point of Pain creates the themes that will play out repeatedly as we walk our path.
- We will encounter those same themes in events, relationships and experiences throughout our life until we confront them.
- Understanding that this is the journey made by every incarnated soul enables us to feel compassion and forgiveness.
- Whatever has happened has been voluntary, intentional and planned prior to incarnation.
- The amnesia triggered fully by our Point of Pain makes us forget this.

WHEN YOU HAVE FORGOTTEN...

Since that time of confusion and pain, when the illusion became real, this echo and its themes have been repeating and replaying in a hundred different ways. It has led to you becoming fearful and wary.

WHEN YOU REMEMBER...

Seeing this as an opportunity to grow, to soften, is new. A tiny seed of hope begins to grow. Maybe you are stronger and braver than you thought. Perhaps you can do this after all.

4

THE ADJUSTMENT

Avoiding: how we try to protect ourselves from further pain, and the consequences of living in fear.

"The signposts have always been there, gentle soul. Are you beginning to see them?"

We stand at a crossroads right now, you and I. Here on this journey together. Looking back, we honour your beginning, all you have gone through. All you knew in those intense early years. The seeds that were sown, and that have since taken root as you walked your path deeper and deeper into forgetting. Looking ahead, we see the road yet to be travelled, the road that will take us all the way to the moment when you are finally free.

> "Life has been harder than you expected. And it has tricked you into closing your heart, and to closing the door to that happiness deep inside you."

While there are still some major hills to climb, these are easier than the mountains you have had to climb earlier. And there will be lush green valleys, the sound of gentle streams, balm for your soul.

The crossroads? These paths off to the side, each in its own way seeming to offer you a better way. They are further roads leading to forgetting. If you go down that one, it will take you into fear. That one in the opposite direction? It leads to anger. More accurately, rage. It is pure aggression, without boundary or empathy. And that third one? That path leads to shame. We all develop a favoured path, one most suited to our personality type, and forged by our life experiences. There were the three basic personality types identified in the ancient Enneagram, a geometric figure originating in Babylon, Greece and Egypt and used to represent a spectrum of personalities. More recently, this figure has been expanded and refined to incorporate nine spiritual personality types by authors such as Russ Hudson and Don Richard Ruso in *The Wisdom of The Enneagram* and Christopher Heuertz's *The Enneagram of Belonging*.

In every moment, you have a choice. You can take any road you wish. You can't get it wrong because the timing of everything is in your own hands. Feel free to go and explore. I'll wait here for you.

As you venture a little way along the road to fear, you'll begin to experience growing anxiety in your body. You will feel increasingly weak, like your legs could give way. There will be a tightness in your chest, and you may feel as if you can't catch your breath. It will become hard to think clearly, as your mind begins to get lost in one story after another – of frightening dramas in which you are helpless to make things safe, and in which terrible scenarios are about to play out.

This is just forgetting, gentle soul. Just sit down where you are and resist the desire to run. There's nothing to run from other than your own imagination. The out-breath will stop this. It will slow it all down and ground you. Come away from the mind and into your body. That's where you can hear your Soul Signature, the totality of all you really are. Come back to presence. The steady out-breath, connecting to the One Breath, remembering that breath is life, and that Life Itself is breathing you.

"Remember, tender soul. Let yourself remember that place. It's inside you."

And that other road? The one that leads to rage? By all means, explore it a little. As you go down that path, you will discover that your vision becomes narrower. And the light begins to fade. You will see everyone you meet a potential enemy, out to get you. To wrong you, to control you. To take what's yours. The further down that path you go, the fuller of rage you'll find yourself becoming. You'll go over every minute detail of everything anyone has ever said to you, done to you. Asked of you, wanted from you. Eventually, beneath the anger, you'll experience a tightness in your throat, and your entire body will be full of pain. Shaking from the effort of holding it all.

The way out? The way back? Tears, my friend. Release. Let them flow. Let yourself sob and your entire body collapse. It will be frightening at first, but ease will come.

And then, to the breath. As the tears calm and stillness finds you, let yourself reconnect. Breathing. The One Breath flowing through you. Your Soul Signature making its presence felt. Back to the awareness of being breathed.

And that final road? The one leading to shame? As you walk along that path, you will experience heat in your body and weakness in your limbs. Your mind will begin to be filled with everything you have ever said, thought, done or experienced. It will feel increasingly as if you are looking down a microscope, until you find you have to stop walking because you can no longer see your way ahead. All you will be able to see is the past, and you will feel a great desire to run while finding that you're unable to make your body move.

When this happens, let yourself sit down and become limp. You don't have to fight this, there's nothing you have to defend or protect. The danger is imaginary, not real. Breathe into this feeling and let it begin to simply flow through you. There's relief in movement, in flow. And then, gradually, lay that microscope down and move away. Rather than becoming those experiences, those moments, simply observe yourself experiencing them. They are not you. They never were. They are Life experiencing itself. No more, no less. All life is here, tender soul. What you have witnessed, we all have witnessed. It has touched all and yet defined none. Let it go. Simply let it go.

All is well. All has always been well, just as it always will be. Here you are, and you have survived this. And so much more. I wanted to show you these roads because the temptation to wander down them is strong. At times of momentary clarity, the pull becomes almost irresistible. To diminish yourself. To go back to what has been comfortable for so long. To resist becoming more.

Marianne Williamson has been quoted many times as pointing out that our greatest fear is not that we are powerless, but rather that we are powerful. How true that is right here. Right now. Allowing yourself to be powerful involves so many new ways of being. In particular, it requires that we break through the illusion that we are purely human, weak and feeble, insufficient, incomplete. That we are not enough, don't know enough. Are not wise enough. That is all illusion. All a product of forgetting. But this is the invitation you face, that of reconnecting with your Soul Signature.

"Are you ready? Are you beginning to remember? Do you see yet, in just a brief glimpse, how amazing you really are?"

So this is where we find ourselves. Right here, right now. At this crossroads. You can't go back. You can never unknow what you now know. You know too much to sink back into forgetting. So then, the crossroads. Will you go further? Shall we walk this next length of the road together? We've spent some time talking about who we really are. Our Essence. Our Soul Signature. Now it's time to journey further into the process of becoming human – into the process of forgetting. We're going to do that by considering the way that the Essence we truly are takes on the characteristics of the personality we have incarnated to be for a lifetime. First, let's just touch base and check in.

POCKET REFLECTION

How does it feel to be standing at this crossroads?

What was your response to the different roads? Which ones felt familiar?

> Is there any part of you that wishes you could go back? Or pull out of this journey? If so, why?
>
> What keeps you from leaving?
>
> What will help you to keep going?

If you're ready, I'll explain what this next part of the journey involves.

In this chapter, we're going to do the work of fully understanding the way we try to avoid a repetition of our original Point of Pain. We do this by developing elaborate structures to protect ourselves, often called defences. They're so called because they're designed to defend us from anything that will trigger pain. We often speak of these structures in a negative way – we might, for example, talk about someone being in denial because they won't look at something they don't want to see – but we'd be mistaken. These structures are immensely creative mechanisms designed solely in our service. They are the only reason we can dare to face a human life: we know our pain will be cushioned until such time as we're ready to integrate it and embrace the growth it offers.

Isn't that amazing? When you really think about it? The construction of our defences that protect us from feelings that might otherwise be overwhelming to a child, together with the knowledge – here's a challenging one – that we can leave our body if we so choose. These two factors combined are what make becoming human manageable.

That bit about leaving our body? Well, we've already spoken lots about the way this happens as a regular going and coming back as we approach death. There's further research that supports the belief that, at times of particularly severe trauma, our consciousness – our Soul – can temporarily leave our body.

For years, shamanic practitioners have talked about "Soul Loss" and "Soul Retrieval". These are terms that can easily be misunderstood or misconstrued. Modern-day practitioners such as Sandra Ingerman, author of *Medicine for the Earth* and *Walking in Light*, and Paul Francis in his books *Finding Your Deep Soul* and *Rewilding Yourself* place their practice within two main principles of quantum physics: that reality is made of vibrational and vibrating energy, and that we are intimately and energetically connected to everything else. In addition, since time and space are simply constructs, this means that healing can take place retroactively, proactively and in many dimensions.

The story of the purple dragon which I shared in chapter 4 is an example of this in action, where the woman flying off through the window on the dragon's back retrieves – or, to use a more mainstream term, "integrates" – the part of her that had left to keep itself safe. Those energetic parts which have temporarily split off have done so to hold all the pain and trauma that were too overwhelming in the moment, until such time as the person who experienced them is ready to invite them back in. Inviting them back leads to the sense of wholeness that is part of healing.

> "To heal is to become whole again, brave soul. You have parts of you waiting to come home."

In my work with survivors of abuse, it is a familiar aspect of this work to discover that, at particularly intolerable times, the client will describe to me how they watched what was happening from a distance. Often, this is from the ceiling, or from the top of a cupboard. Sophie told me:

I would listen out in the dark for the familiar creaking of the floorboard just outside my bedroom door. I would always know it was him, because he would be walking on tiptoe, carefully, so my mother wouldn't hear him and wake up.

I could always smell the drink on his breath as he opened the door.

As he got into bed with me, I would become aware of the silence, of ceasing to feel anything at all. It was like I was in a soundless tunnel, where everything became distorted. I knew what was about to happen, but it was as if a part of me was already no longer there.

I would find myself leaving at speed, to realize that I was watching from the top of the cupboard. I could see what was happening but could feel nothing. The body that was me in the bed was numb, beyond pain. I watched what was happening but was untouched by it.

Afterwards, when he'd gone, I seemed to be back in my body, but with no recollection of what had happened. It's only as we work together now, and I find these memories coming back to me, that I'm able to tell you this.

In his book *The Body Says No*, ground-breaking trauma specialist Gabor Maté gives a comprehensive overview of such mechanisms. It is one of the most comforting truths that loved ones can hold in mind when agonizing over something that someone close has gone through. All is not necessarily how it seems. I have had many fascinating discussions about what energy workers know as soul loss, and psychologists and psychotherapists know as dissociation. Since I straddle both camps, the conclusion I inevitably reach is an energetic one, since everything is – unquestionably – energy vibrating. In her fascinating book *From Quantum Physics to Energy Healing*, Dr Johanna Blomqvist shows how there are significant elements of quantum physics in ancient Eastern philosophy – especially Vedanta – and in much Buddhist philosophy, as well as in shamanic beliefs the world over.

Such research represents a significant change in perception about healing: an understanding of these processes, therefore, which focusses on the way the energy that is the soul makes use of the systems of the body and brain, as opposed to a more mechanistic view based upon the idea that experience and consciousness are situated in the brain and body.

POCKET REFLECTION

Take some time to reflect on what we've considered in this chapter so far. What has struck you especially?

Are there things you find yourself struggling with? Puzzled by? Needing to take time to work out or find your way through?

How did you experience that word "forgive"? It's a word that can bring all sorts of emotions, so just let them arise.

What about that suggestion that you might need to forgive yourself? We experience all sorts of reactions to that possibility. What is yours?

What have you got to forgive yourself for? If anything? It could be that you want to say nothing. Or to say it can never be forgiven. Or something else?

Now think about how it felt to hear the suggestion that you might find it easier to forgive someone else? Who came to mind? How did it feel?

How are you right now? What do you need?

Do that. Either in reality or in your imagination. Everything is energy and is now. Do what you need to do.

> Write down in your Healing Journal how that felt. And what else you might need to do.

ADJUSTING TO PAIN

Let's have a look next at how we adjust to living with pain. Or, to put it more accurately, how we adjust – or modify – pain to make it survivable. Talking in depth about the psychological and emotional effects of trauma, and its impact on the systems of the body and its energy systems, is outside the remit and purpose of this book. Our purpose here is to focus on the bigger picture, to step right back and to find an accessible way to work with what we've known in a way that allows us to observe its effects and find a way to go beyond those effects in order to heal.

> "You are the observer, stand back and you can see more clearly."

So I'm going to generalize for a moment. I'm going to focus on the four ways we human beings react to having encountered pain. They are the four trauma responses of fight, flight, freeze and fawn (sometimes called appease). Those four ways, in turn, tend to be adopted by four different kinds of personalities. And those four types of personalities tend to have formed, as I have observed over the years, in response to particular sorts of environments in which certain kinds of experiences have taken place in the company of certain types of people surrounding us.

Let's take some time out to get up to speed with those four types of trauma responses …

THE FIGHT RESPONSE

To fight is to confront a threat or danger aggressively. If this is how you have dealt with traumatic pain, then:

- You tend to anticipate threat and danger even where there is none.
- You are easily cynical and suspicious, tending to believe others have ulterior motives.
- You believe everyone is in it for themselves and out to get you.
- You go on the attack rather than seek compromise or negotiation.
- You believe that being strong means not giving in, not admitting when you are wrong and never saying sorry.
- You believe that showing your feelings is a sign of weakness, and tend to despise those who do.
- You state opinions as if they are facts, and believe that anyone who doesn't see things the way you do is wrong.
- You blame others when things go wrong, and for causing whatever feeling you are experiencing.
- You always expect a battle, so go into situations on the attack rather than expecting the other person to be willing to be reasonable.
- You tend to hold concepts like "you made me feel" as opposed to "I felt this" – so never consider your own contribution to what happens.
- You tend to be rigid and fixed, unwilling to consider new ideas or to change your opinion or behaviour.

THE FLIGHT RESPONSE

To take flight is to run from a threat or danger. If this is how you have dealt with traumatic pain, then:

- You avoid any situation that makes you feel uncomfortable.

- You will always try to persuade someone else to speak for you or to stand up for you.
- You can be manipulative and try to make others feel protective toward you.
- You often present yourself as the victim in a situation and make others feel sorry for you.
- You are passive, believing that there's little you can do to change anything.
- You are afraid to stand up for yourself, or for others, believing that it will always go badly.
- You tend to hold a fatalistic view of life: what will be will be.
- You hold a lot of secret resentment, envy even, toward the lives others have and what others have achieved.
- You see unfairness and injustice everywhere, even where others have simply achieved through their own hard work and effort.

THE FREEZE RESPONSE

To freeze is to experience paralysis or an inability to think or act when faced with a threat or danger. If this is how you have dealt with traumatic pain, then:

- You find your mind going blank whenever something feels uncomfortable.
- People might describe you unkindly as being like a rabbit caught in the headlights.
- You experience a great deal of fear if invited to step outside your comfort zone.
- You struggle to find words when you feel under any kind of pressure.
- When frightened, you experience time as slowing down, as if you are caught in a moment that seems to go on forever.
- You can feel as if you are not in your body, and therefore unable to make it move or respond, or feel anything.

- This can become a response you find yourself falling into in the face of any threat, real or perceived, external or in your mind or imagination.

THE FAWN (APPEASE) RESPONSE

To fawn or appease is to respond by complying with, or protecting, the person posing the threat in an attempt to save yourself. If this is how you have dealt with traumatic pain, then:

- You adapt your behaviour to fit in with however others want you to be (or what you believe them to want).
- You have trouble identifying what you feel or want, because you're always trying to work out what you should feel or want.
- You tend to feel like you don't know who you are.
- You spend a lot of time playing out different scenarios, what you should have said, what you wish you'd done.
- You tend to dread conflict and avoid it at all costs.
- When faced with someone angry or challenging, your first instinct is to appease them.
- You often think of yourself as weak or cowardly.
- You override your own beliefs, truths, wishes and accept instead those of people around you.
- You tend to agree with and support what others think and say, and remain passive when asked for your opinion, usually saying you don't know or don't mind.
- You tend to experience moods you can't explain throughout the day, and often feel at the mercy of your emotions.
- You live in your imagination a lot of the time, and your mind tends to create dramas and catastrophes which you find yourself getting lost in.
- You feel angry at yourself and find ways to punish yourself, often by denying yourself kindness or things you would enjoy.

- You tend to find it hard to say no, and people often put on you without realizing that you mind.
- You feel threatened and exposed if someone asks you for an opinion in case others disagree and you feel judged.
- You fear others' judgement above all else and go to great lengths to avoid this.
- You make yourself as invisible as possible, as helpful as possible and as undemanding as possible.
- You tend to identify with your feelings, and with what has happened to you, believing that these define you.

It feels important to say that every single one of these adaptive responses to trauma is generated automatically. There is no blame or judgement called for here, and certainly none intended. We're here to heal, and healing involves becoming familiar with what's happened to us in the process of forgetting our true nature and power so that we can go beyond once more into remembering.

What's interesting – and significant for our purpose – is that the same situation can produce a different response in different people. More accurately, in different souls. The particular response isn't inevitable. It's variable depending on the potential characteristics of the personality with which we have chosen to incarnate, and the environment we have similarly chosen to experience.

ADJUSTING THE VOLUME

Let's bring back one of the people we've already met briefly before. I'm going to talk about him in the way we're learning to become more comfortable with: that of a soul here voluntarily to experience a human lifetime. Remember Josh? And the incident with the water hose?

So you'll recall that one of the members of his Soul Family who agreed to incarnate with Josh took the role of his father. For the purpose of this lifetime, this Soul Family member voluntarily adopted the personality of an anxious man, given to outbursts of rage and unpredictable behaviour. As part of his own preparation for incarnation, Josh chose to adopt a sensitive and loving personality. You'll recall that, because of this particular choice, Josh's response to his father's temperament and behaviour was to come to believe that the fault lay with him. That if he were more tuned in and careful to his father's moods and needs, he could avert his father's outbursts. So Josh developed the fourth strategy: he learned to appease.

However, turn the volume up, intensify the experience of the Set-Up, and Josh could have chosen to incarnate in order to experience standing up to his father, taking him on. In this case, he'd be far more likely to respond to his father's rage with matching indignation and outrage. In this case, we'd see the fight response.

Turn the volume down, choose a different Set-Up again, and we could observe a Josh who had chosen to experience a father who was far more intimidating. A thug and a bully, who set out to break him. A far tougher challenge. An even greater opportunity for growth and becoming more. In this scenario, we might well see a Josh experiencing a flight response. Learning to try to avoid trouble by becoming as invisible as possible, keeping his head down. Avoiding rather than confronting.

Turn the volume right up, nearly as high as it will go, and Josh might have invited that member of his Soul Family to become an abuser. To threaten his sense of safety in some way – a combination of physical, psychological, sexual abuse, abandonment and neglect. This would present Josh with the most intense and challenging experience of all. But through that experience he would find opportunities for growth he would find nowhere else. His likely response in a situation like this? Freeze.

Shall we take some time at this point to have one of our sit-downs together? Bits of the journey are particularly hard, aren't they? New ideas are especially challenging. But think about it – everything I've just described is entirely in keeping with the research findings we've shared earlier. It's just that we've suddenly gone a step further and made them real. Happening to a real person. Someone who could be you. Or me. Or anyone of us. But is, in fact, all of us. As is Josh's father. In Oneness, what happens to one happens to all. And what one does, we all do. And by now, you'll know what I'm going to say next: when one heals, we all heal.

POCKET REFLECTION

What do you find yourself recognizing in yourself as you read this chapter?

What do these realizations tell you about what kinds of pain, or whose behaviour or hurts, you're feeling a need to defend yourself against?

What are you afraid might happen if you let that defence go? Can you? Is it true?

How might you face things in a more helpful way?

How do you let yourself heal from this by being real instead?

THE TRIANGLE OF INSIGHT

For the purpose of this journey, going forward, we're going to focus particularly on the three major emotions which we'll find underneath every single one of the categories and characteristics we've considered above. Those roads off the main path we talked about earlier. Let me remind you what they are: rage, fear, shame.

We're going to think about them in a really different way. We're going to look at one of the fundamental truths about healing that will help you. It's this: all pain is memory pain. That's because all pain is actually a retriggering of our original point of pain. We meet that pain repeatedly in different forms and from different angles.

What we don't so readily appreciate is that sometimes we even swap roles and cause that same pain in someone else. Remember the saying "hurt people hurt people"? Never a truer word. We tend to think of that in a negative way. And, of course, I'm not for a moment suggesting that it's ever something we want to do. At least, mostly, let's be honest. But when that does happen – when we do act unkindly or let someone down – if we're willing and open, we get offered a moment of possible reflection. Because we can factor in what we've learned about why we behaved that way and apply some of that insight to a greater understanding of what might have been behind the actions of those who did the same to us. Do you see how everything is always working out, and always inviting us to heal?

"We are always being invited to heal, and things are always working themselves out."

So let's go back to trauma and its effects. Trauma is about feeling unsafe, remember. When faced with feeling unsafe, a child has really only three possible responses: rage, fear and shame. These are the same three possible responses we continue to experience throughout our adult life whenever those old hurts are rekindled. Margaret Wilkinson, a past tutor in my psychotherapy training, explains the "kindling response" in

Changing Minds in Therapy: Emotion, Attachment, Trauma and Neurobiology, building on the work of American psychologist Allan Schore into dissociative responses. She describes vividly the sensations every one of us will recognize that take place in the body as old memories are made live again by a seemingly unrelated incident in the present. We experience a sudden electric shock, a tingling surging through our body, followed by being unable momentarily to think. We're catapulted back in time, it's as if there is no time, we've gone beyond time. And we're caught in a moment of recalling the full impact of the original as if it's happening now but in relation to this situation.

One of the most helpful truths we can come to understand is the true nature of these experiences. We tend to refer to ourselves as having been "triggered" but it's natural to assume that it's the current situation that has triggered us. We feel frustrated and annoyed with ourselves for being so easily upset or frightened by something we feel shouldn't have this power to affect us. That's because it always feels so much more extreme than the situation appears to warrant. This is due to the "kindling response": something in the current situation is sufficiently similar to the original situation that it set off a neurobiological process. That process throws us into the original state of high arousal and traumatic response which the original experience engendered.

What if we don't know where our trauma originated?

This is something people ask a lot. Especially at the outset of a healing journey. They know they have strong reactions to certain people, events or situations. I understand how bewildering this can feel. I'm going to share with you how I, as a psychotherapist, go about helping people to work this out.

When I was in training, one of the most valuable tools I was given was the understanding that everything that happens in the room with me will also be happening out there in the person's life; and will also have happened back in earlier years. In here, out there, back then: this is known in therapy as the "triangle of insight". We show each other what we've known without even needing to do anything very much at all. We all live those experiences out in our body language, in our voice, in our behaviour. In our very way of being, as the next story makes clear.

BELLA'S STORY

Bella knocks hesitantly at my front door and stands right back as I open it, apologizing that she's a few minutes early. She tells me she'd always rather be early than late. She asks me how I am and seems unduly worried to reassure herself that I am okay and up to seeing her today. If not, she can always come back a different day.

As Bella comes into my hallway, she asks if I want her to take her shoes off. I say no, it's fine. She insists on taking them off anyway, and then picks them up and carries them with her into the therapy room. She sits on the edge of her seat and keeps her coat on, placing her shoes neatly arranged next to her feet.

When I invite her to tell me a little about what has brought her here, she tries several times to speak, fighting tears and brushing them away angrily. She shakes her head and apologizes for getting upset. She says she knew she would get upset and says sorry several times. She tells me what she's come about is such a little thing, that I must see people all the time with problems far greater than hers. She shouldn't have troubled me. She's just being silly.

Already, I'm sure, you've picked up a lot about Bella. Let me tell you what I would see straight away that would give me a window into Bella's point of pain. You'll have seen some of this too. To go back to the triangle of insight that I mentioned earlier, in here:

- Bella is more concerned about me than herself.
- She mustn't trouble me with her problems.

- She mustn't leave her mess around (her shoes, but also her "emotional mess" – she apologizes for crying).
- Bella is worried about whether I'm in a good enough place to manage her pain (she asks me several times if I'm okay and offers to come back another time if I'm not strong enough today).
- Bella has learned that she shouldn't cry (she apologizes when she does).
- She has learned to minimize her own pain because other people's pain is much worse.
- Bella walks through the world trying to make as little impact as possible and always apologizing for herself, her feelings and her needs.

This is borne out by Bella's "out there" story, which is about always being put upon and taken for granted and never being able to ask for help or say no.

This is further borne out by Bella's "back then" story, which Bella eventually gets to reluctantly because she doesn't want to appear selfish or a bad person. Bella's mother was a perfectionist, always needing everything to be just so. There could be no "mess" of any kind. This included emotional and psychological mess and meant that Bella was encouraged always to cheer up, realize things weren't that bad really, and to think just how lucky she was.

Do you see how our pain leaks through? All these years later, here is Bella still acting that old pain out. And she's repeated all that learning with her children, too. She makes no demands on them, never talks about her own needs, puts few boundaries in place, and experiences the hurt of not being seen or considered all over again. Bella struggles hugely with shame and is forever trying to prevent herself from experiencing it by making herself as small, unobtrusive and invisible as she possibly can.

Pain is always memory pain. Any situation or event in our adult life that evokes an enormous physical response is doing so because it has rekindled an original source of trauma. One of the most difficult things to manage, in the light of this, is a trauma response that happened before we could think about it – that is, trauma that is pre-verbal. However, even if we can't put words to the memory, our body tells us it exists, and it deserves the same compassionate acceptance and tender care.

If we understand trauma, our ways of dealing with it, our various responses to it, and the way it gets endlessly retriggered, then we have some ways of getting to grips with what happens to us – and in us – in those moments when we feel like we're out of control. When we feel we have lost ourselves. This is one of the greatest challenges we spiritual beings here for a human experience on Planet Earth face.

"Every human being has known trauma, and each one of us is on a journey to heal."

It's the big one, the core challenge. Everything flows from the experience of trauma and healing involves recovering from it.

One further thought is helpful: the Essence that we are is never traumatized. Our Soul Signature remains intact throughout. It stays available at all times; it is our true nature and who we always are. So then, what is traumatized? Or more accurately, what part of us has experienced the trauma? It is the personality we have adopted for this lifetime. This form. This body, this brain, this energy system. The part of our energy that incarnated for the adventure. Our Soul Signature is untouched because our Soul Signature never loses its true nature.

POCKET REFLECTION

Where has all this left you? What's going on in you right now? What pain has been rekindled? What memories came to the surface as you read?

Remember that you have survived. That all has happened to help you grow, become more.

Remind yourself that you are far braver than you believe – you know this simply because you chose to incarnate for these challenges. What courage that takes!

Jot down in your Healing Journal the things you've come to realize and any questions you still have.

Decide what you need right now. Do that.

HOW WE HEAL

Let's go back to one of the startling facts that has come out of that research we looked at earlier into lives between lives. You'll recall that we only incarnate with a small percentage of our Essence, our total energetic "beingness". If you'd lost sight of that bit, it might be helpful to refer back before reading on (see page 49). It might have seemed a small detail at the time, one you maybe even missed, but in terms of healing, it's everything. To heal is to recover the awareness of our true nature. It's to recover the ability to be aware and to observe, rather than to be immersed in the illusion of the movie we seem to be in.

So the more we can understand what's happened to us as being a consequence of incarnation and of forgetting, the better able we are to free ourselves from the effects of trauma by understanding how it works; and the better we get at reconnecting with our Soul Signature rather than our adopted personality; and the more we become familiar with managing this body and brain and energy system rather than feeling at its mercy, the more successfully we can restore ourselves and heal. Because we will finally begin to remember. And once we remember, once we heal, then we free ourselves to live joyfully, compassionately and wisely, with a degree of resilience and inner strength that will become a beacon for others, and a source of comfort and certainty for ourselves.

So back to that kindling response, the electric shock, the huge wave of anxiety, the inability to think, the sense of being caught in a moment that could last forever. What to do? How to find a way to move beyond so you can connect with your Soul Signature? The major part of you? How do you reconnect with Oneness? How can you re-establish yourself as the observer rather than becoming submerged as the experiencer? Witness the part of you experiencing rather than identifying with it? How do you remember?

USING THE BREATH

You can remember and reconnect with Oneness by using stillness and the breath. Instead of becoming the storm, you notice that the storm is happening, and you breathe into it. Through it. It is energy only. You are not this storm happening in your body and in your mind. You are the awareness that is witnessing it. And beyond and within this moment, there is an even greater awareness: the field of creative, unconditionally loving, all-embracing consciousness of which you are a part. Also witnessing, also aware. Let yourself feel that, becoming still and being the noticer. You are not this body, nor this response. You are not this brain, which so often becomes blank and unable to think, or speeded up and agitated, with a flurry of random thoughts scattering all meaning.

"You are not this body, nor this response. You are the soul experiencing and noticing. All is well."

You are the breath. Take normal breaths in, long breaths out, increasingly slow and steady. Concentrate on the breath only. Don't try to take on the mind; in this moment you can't. Not yet. Still the body's trauma response first. The out-breath in particular does this. The mind will try to invite you to engage with it, wanting to pull you into the drama. To persuade you to fight, to flee. To become paralysed. To try to bargain, negotiate. To argue, to try to overpower it. You can do that later. After. Not now. The mind can't hear you.

But the body is listening, and the body will respond to the breath. Always. Check that the mind doesn't catch you in the headlights, make you hold your breath, or take shallow breaths. That will lead to you believing you can't breathe, because your lungs will be full of air, which you will interpret as not being able to breathe. You can. You simply breathe out. Breathe. And then, gradually, let yourself be breathed. Closing your eyes may help.

Connect. Plug in. Until you experience a different kind of sensation: energy beginning to flow. You'll feel it in your hands. Or your legs. Or as a strange sensation on the top of your head, as if something is playing with your hair. Or there might be a sensation like tickling on your face, or the back of your neck. Keep breathing. Join with the breath, become it. It will steady you, hold you. Become aware of being aware.

ASCEND IN YOUR SACRED SPACE

Using your word or phrase of intention, bring yourself to your Sacred Space. *Be here now.*

Let your breath slow, settle into a steady rhythm. All is well with you. In this place you are safe. There is no blame. No shame. No failure. There is only wisdom and learning.

Settle yourself comfortably, preferably sitting down. Look around you at this Sacred Space. Familiarize yourself again with its shapes and colours, textures and sounds.

You realize that you rarely look up. You do so now. At the ceiling or the sky, whatever form this takes. Pause for a moment to take in the shapes and patterns above you. The light and shadow. Focus on the interplay of forms that you see there.

As you watch and explore with your eyes, you realize that it is your consciousness itself which is doing the looking. You discover that, although you are still on the ground, your consciousness can go anywhere you wish.

You enjoy this discovery for a while. It's fun and freeing. One moment you're looking at everything through a microscope, the next you're panning right out to take in everything around you. You see intricate patterns, mesmerized by their complexity. You touch different textures and surfaces, marvelling at the detail. Then you sweep back and zoom out across the whole scene. It's exhilarating to understand that you're in no way imprisoned in your body.

Then, as you look up once more, you see a series of steps leading upwards further than you can see. Beyond the roof or canopy. Right up into the sky. Curious, you decide to investigate.

You climb for a long way. The steps seem now to be set into rock. You can tell by how worn away these rocks are that many feet have come this way.

The higher you climb, the more you realize you are entering silence. Not a frightening silence; it feels immensely peaceful. You might even say sacred. You are puzzled, yet eager to see where this leads.

Finally, the landscape levels out. You see ahead of you a cave set into rock. You know this is where you're meant to go.

As you approach, you notice there are candles burning within this place. Reaching the entrance, you see that the cave is far bigger than the entrance suggests. The ceiling towers above you and the cave seems to extend back into what you realize is a mountainside.

Around the inside of this place there are shelves of scrolls. From floor to ceiling, all rolled neatly and laying one on top of another. You seem to be at the entrance to a library. It's bigger than any library you have ever known. You notice a strange vibration in the air; like a low hum. A soothing sound. It reaches right inside you.

A beam of light suddenly falls on one particular scroll. It is set apart, on a table at one side. In the same moment that the beam of light appears, you hear footsteps approaching from deep inside the cave. Light emanates from whoever this is, growing in intensity as they get closer.

And then, they are here. In this room. The figure wears a cloak, and a hood hides their face. Yet you feel no alarm. The figure's energy is tangible. Loving and serene.

They walk over to the scroll on which the beam of light is resting, pick it up, and, to your surprise, approach you. As they get closer, they pull back the hood of their robe. You catch your breath.

The face you see is startling. An old face, ancient. A face that has known thousands of years of pain and joy, sorrow and beauty. There is such gentle wisdom in the eyes. You feel known and understood. This figure sees you. Fully.

They walk up to you, holding the scroll in both hands. The eyes hold yours for a moment. Then, with a bow of the head, they offer you the scroll. As they look up again, you see that they are smiling. There are tears in their eyes. You find that you have tears in yours also. Then, without warning, the figure is gone. So is the light that accompanied them. Only the candlelight remains.

For some time, you stand transfixed, full of an emotion you can't name. Then you remember the scroll. Sitting down near the entrance, where there is light to see more clearly, you begin to unfurl it.

You are astonished to see that the scroll doesn't contain writing, as you'd expected. It is filled with scenes from your past; they have a life of their own. You see yourself being born; the young child you were. Everything is here.

Not only *your* story, but everyone else's too. Everyone you have ever known is in here. You watch as your life is played out; some parts you remember, some you had forgotten. Others you were unaware of. You discover that you can also go back and forth, playing out different versions, seeing what might have happened. You immerse yourself in this amazing experience, watching with fascination.

You realize you are watching this person who is clearly you from a different perspective. It's as if you're watching but engaged at the same time. You can feel this person's feelings, hear their thoughts and follow their actions and choices; yet you're also removed, observing and learning from all you're seeing.

And then, you feel a presence and realize the figure has returned. In the tenderest gesture, the figure bends down, places a hand on your head, and speaks your name. You look up in surprise: again the gentle compassion; that deepest knowing.

You realize they are asking for the scroll, and you release it. As the figure takes it from you, they reach into a pocket of their gown and place an object in your hands. Then, in a moment, the figure, the scroll, the cave are gone; you are here in your Sacred Space, your hands tight around the gift you were given.

Finding somewhere comfortable to sit, you open your hands to see what this object is. What do you see? It has personal meaning for you. You ponder what has happened for some time. You want to remember every detail, hold it close.

Finally you're ready. You get up and place this object on your altar. Then, just before you leave, you do something you have never done before. It feels significant now.

You stand before this altar you have created, on which there are so many items that represent the journey you are making.

For the first time, you look at it all in awe. With love; with admiration.

And you bow.

When you feel ready, share your feelings and thoughts with your Healing Journal.

POCKET TAKEAWAYS

- We adjust to trauma (our Point of Pain) by creating defences against further pain.
- Our defences are not wrong, they have helped us to survive.
- Our defences protect us, but also reinforce the illusions we come to believe are true as a result of our traumatic experiences.
- By protecting us from feeling, our defences also limit our ability to experience joy, love, compassion and true freedom.
- Eventually, this leads to our becoming aware that we are unhappy and dissatisfied.
- This leads to our search for healing.

WHEN YOU HAVE FORGOTTEN...

We had always thought of triggers – and something bad. We were taught that we should be over it by now, should forgive. That we should just be able to let it go.

WHEN YOU REMEMBER...

Seeing them as an opportunity to grow, to soften, is new. Instead of triggers being bad, we can now begin to see that they are signposts to what needs healing, and the path to true peace and freedom.

5

THE CRISIS

Crisis: the event that catapults us back in time
to confront and heal our original trauma.

"If ever there was a time to
hold your nerve, courageous soul,
it's now."
"You are so very close.
Just keep walking."

So here we are, at the crossroads on our journey. We've looked at where you originate from, and who you really are. We've thought together about how that came to be, what happened before you came, and why you decided to make this journey on Planet Earth. We've explored the early challenges you've encountered; and we've examined the stories that have arisen out of those. We've considered the alternative routes of rage, fear and shame. We've marvelled at the ways you have managed to survive this time–space experience up to the present time; and we've celebrated your bravery and resourcefulness in getting to this moment. So, what next? We've arrived at the Crisis.

This is one of the most challenging points in our journey. It always involves a complete stripping away of all we thought we were, knew, could trust and rely on. It is the time when the veil is at its most opaque, and all sense of safety is ripped away. There's nowhere to go except inwards. The world – in which we have forgotten who we really are, and all that we are truly forever connected to – has offered us its most bitter taste of duality, and we are now being invited to reach deep inside and reconnect with our Soul Signature.

> "Dig deep, lovely one. Just keep walking and the way will appear. Always and every time. Feel the love that surrounds you now."

It's time to bring together everything that's happened up to this point. Because nothing has been accidental, nothing random. There has been pattern and purpose in everything, and all of it has been leading you here. No one comes to this point without going through some big stuff. And no one goes beyond it into healing without facing that stuff and moving through it. They are the experiences that led you to look in this book, to reach for more, to recognize the need for relief and healing. That process has now reached a point of no return.

The Crisis is the point at which current experiences or events break us open in such a way that our original Point of Pain becomes once again raw and exposed. We can no longer avoid dealing with what we have been avoiding for so long. The Crisis is a healing crisis: do we allow ourselves to go through the process that will lead to healing, or do we stay where we are?

This moment will look different for each of us. We often describe it as "the straw that broke the camel's back". It's accompanied by a feeling that says, "I can't go through this again", or a recognition that says, "How have I found myself here yet again?" It's the moment when we finally notice that a particular experience has kept repeating, in slightly different forms, throughout our entire life: the experience we incarnated in order to encounter, to fully engage with, and from which we are finally ready to heal.

The intention at the heart of this book – its message and its method – has been to try to illuminate the spiral path we journey along, in order to help us see our way more clearly; to illustrate its predictable milestones and, in so doing, help us to identify our own. Far from trying to soften or oversimplify, it's felt important to stay honest and real about what it's like to live this human life. To acknowledge what it is to become fully human while still being fully divine, in a way similar to that celebrated by Amoda Maa Jeevan in her wonderful book *Embodied Enlightenment*. To refuse, if you like, the temptation to collude together in what John Welwood, in his book *Toward a Psychology of Awakening*, talks of what he terms the "spiritual bypass". The quick fix, the magic wand, the sticking plaster over the open wound.

One of the biggest challenges we ever face – and it happens to every single one of us sooner or later – is the Crisis that finally brings us to the crossroads we explored earlier, on the path that leads to healing. The Crisis can be, and usually is, excruciating.

It brings us face to face starkly with everything we've spent years running from or trying not to acknowledge. It's the point at which we realize we can't ignore these things any longer.

Any guide who claims to be willing to go with us through the complex human journey toward spiritual awakening, and the healing transformation that lies beyond, but fails at some point to address the enormity of this crisis, is doing us a disservice and facilitating what is merely a spiritual bypass. We may feel a bit better temporarily – at least until we hit a crisis – but we certainly won't be healed.

It's so easy to walk the smoother, less strenuous, path; the one that claims that we can just think ourselves happy, avoid pain, transform any experience into something heart-numbingly positive, rationalize and intellectualize away the true nature of what it means to be human; that is opting for that spiritual bypass. So many of us fall for it initially – it appears so inviting. But it's the way of the head, not the heart. Its source is the ego because its focus is on individual acquisition: "I deserve" and "I want" and "me, me, me". Heart-centred living doesn't sound like that, neither does it feel like that. Oneness isn't found there. Neither is spiritual resilience.

> "In reality, lovely one, we're not stuck; we're just afraid. The pain is about to dissolve. Keep going."

So then the Crisis happens: an event, an experience, an encounter with a person (familiar to us or sometimes a stranger) propels us into a place where we're forced to confront everything we've been running from up to this point. There's no going back; but at the time it can feel as if there's no way to go forward, either.

What can feel so unnerving about the Crisis, also, is that it so often occurs when we finally believe we've got this thing called

Life well and truly worked out. We've nailed it and we're on our way. And then, seemingly out of nowhere, we fall flat on our face – and we didn't even see it coming. Here are some of the typical signs that we have hit the Crisis:

- We experience profound self-doubt, and find ourselves calling into question everything we ever thought or believed.
- The pain associated with whatever the trigger that catapulted us into this state feels raw, excruciating, as if we can hardly bear it.
- We live in a haze of unprocessed emotion, triggered by anything and everyone.
- We lose interest in life, weighed down by the weight of all we're suddenly having to deal with.
- We swing between being tearful, feeling angry and slipping into dark depression.
- Our Point of Pain re-emerges, the memory of it complete and undiluted, as if we're living it right now, all over again.
- We begin to see the repeating patterns in our life: both things that have happened, and the way we have dealt with them.
- We feel desperate for relief and healing but don't know how or where to find it.

When the Crisis first hits, we often flounder. We weren't prepared for this; it wasn't supposed to go this way. What were we doing wrong that we attracted this? Where did we slip up? Maybe it was our thoughts of lack? Perhaps we didn't believe hard enough?

It isn't any of those. Truly it isn't. Let it go – stop beating yourself up here. All that's happening is that you've hit the place you always came for. And you are doing it so well. It brought you here, and we're going to go through to the other side. At any point you can take a break; we don't have to walk a certain distance a day. We don't have to walk at a set speed, to cover a set amount of ground by a specified date. You can sit down and rest whenever you like; and you might also like to build in some regular journaling time, space for reflection and meditation. You might like to go back over old ground, read bits again, contemplate them some more.

POCKET REFLECTION

Reflect on what has brought you here, to this point. Allow yourself to wander over old ground – the steep and rugged parts, the gentler times.

The ways in which your point of pain has brought you on this journey to now ...

The trigger/issue that finally proved to be the catalyst, setting you on this road ...

Notice what feelings and sensations are arising in you as you visit these things.

What hopes and what fears are present right now?

THE DARK NIGHT

When you feel you're refreshed and ready, we're going to think more together about the Crisis that brought you to this point. How it arose, what it means, where it leads if you'll allow it to show you. In the meantime, let's take a tiny detour for a moment to talk about the "Dark Night of the Soul". It's a term first attributed to a Spanish friar, John of the Cross, in the 16th century. Many writers since have underlined the accuracy of that phrase in describing the Crisis, both human and spiritual, which always precedes the evolving process we call spiritual awakening. That process is different for each of us; but it's a process not an event. Here's how it went for John of the Cross.

Juan de la Cruz (later known as John) experienced a terrifying sense of abandonment, separation and bleakness that he could not find his way out of for a long time. It was nothing short of an existential crisis. Following a traumatic childhood (more on that shortly), Juan entered the Church and became a friar in the strict Carmelite Order.

Through this, he met St Teresa of Avila, a Carmelite nun, and was greatly influenced by her reforming beliefs, which resulted in her setting up and placing him in charge of her first "reform convent". However, the mainstream Carmelites, threatened by what they regarded as heresy, captured and imprisoned him. He was kept in a tiny cell, not even big enough to lie down in. Twice a day he was taken out and flogged. The rest of the time he spent cold and shivering in the dark. In the winter it was freezing; in the summer it was sweltering. At all times it was claustrophobic, the only tiny window being high above his head, giving insufficient light to see. The monks would torture him by speaking in whispers outside the cell door, telling him that no one cared about him, that everyone had abandoned him and it was as if he hadn't ever even existed.

In his *The Spiritual Canticle*, John of the Cross – more recently given the title Saint, and one of the greatest contemplative mystics and visionaries of all time – takes us through the terror and brutal anguish of his imprisonment to a place of pure presence, love and peace, and transformation. In "Dark Night of the Soul", he writes: "Even though this holy night darkens the spirit, it does so only to light up everything."

In recent times, the phrase "dark night of the soul" has sometimes been medicalized, being seen as something similar to depression. In fact, that is very far from its actual nature. It is the healing crisis, the breaking through, the experience of losing all we thought we knew and were, the beginning of the process which leads us from forgetting back to remembering. Everything we have relied on, all we have held dear or true, dissolves away, together with our sense of safety and trust. It brings us to a point of agonizing aloneness, where all meaning seems to have disintegrated and we have no idea how to go on, or who we will be when we go on.

However, while this phrase – and the experience it describes so well – tends to be applied to a very particular existential crisis, often within a narrow definition with religious connotations, I want to show you a much broader application. Remember the concept of "in here, out there, back then" that I introduced briefly you to in chapter 5? (See page 115.) Let's apply that to John of the Cross and see what we learn.

John of the Cross suffered his "dark night" as a direct result of the experience of incarceration we just talked about. And, of course, wouldn't those experiences plunge anyone into such a place? But let's now dig deeper still. Let's look for the repeat. The Point of Pain prior to the Crisis. What isn't generally added into the mix – possibly because it has never seemed relevant – is the way in which his experience of being incarcerated and beaten, humiliated and made to believe everyone had abandoned him, losing everything he'd known and relied on to that point, and the enormous life change this precipitated, was a direct repeat in a different form of what he had known as a boy. This is where it gets particularly relevant for our purposes, because:

- John's father was an accountant, belonging to and working within a wealthy family of accountants.
- This family disowned John's father when he chose to marry a woman from a poorer working class.
- As a result of their poverty, John's family suffered and knew the restriction and loss that comes with losing everything.

- John's father died when John was three years old, and
  his little brother Luis died two years after that, most likely
  from malnutrition.
- John's mother found work as a weaver, but John was sent
  to a boarding school for poor and orphaned children.

So we're talking trauma: the family's fall from grace and
consequent stigma; poverty and malnutrition; the loss of his
father; the loss of his brother; the toll this would all have taken
on his mother and the effect of that on John; being sent away
at not much older than five years of age, with the loss of all
he had known. And the inevitable harshness and cruelty of an
orphanage regime, where I have no doubt that shivering – an
unmistakable trauma reaction – originated. It doesn't take much
empathy or imagination, does it, to begin to realize that – far
from being the original instigator of John's dark night – it was
the trigger, the Crisis, which rekindled his original trauma. And
in doing so, it opened the portal to his healing journey.

Mirabai Starr, author of *Saint John of The Cross: Devotions,
Prayers and Living Wisdom* and her more personal and intimate
Caravan of No Despair: A Memoir of Loss and Transformation, in
which she shares the journey through her own dark night of the
soul, which began the day her daughter died, is one of the most
influential proponents and interpreters of the works of St John of
the Cross. She makes what I feel is such an accurate observation
of the current times we live in, when she suggests that, as an
entire planet, we are going through a Dark Night of the Soul.

She isn't alone in seeing these increasingly turbulent times in
this way. As I write, the entire world remains in the grip of a
global pandemic, global warming is of pressing concern, there
is increasing activism based around inequality and injustice, and
widespread political unrest. The world needs visionaries,
peacemakers and healers as never before, as we travel ever
nearer toward the point of crisis and the invitation it's offering

us. And so, to anyone choosing to incarnate at this time, and to be part of this process, brave you are for sure. Thank you.

> "We really are all in this together, just walking each other home. Weary, scarred, hurting, but with swelling hearts and deepening courage. In love and Oneness."

So now, back to John of the Cross. We understand better the link between "in here, back then". And the "out there"? Well, John was a rebel and fighter for social justice, a reformer within his own Carmelite Order, finding himself frequently imprisoned for his outspoken challenge to authority, its disregard for suffering and failure to help the poor and disinherited. Do you see the spiral? The repeats? The way it all ends up coming full circle? Do you see the Soul Path, and how it led to crisis, breakthrough and ultimate healing?

Not all of us would feel inclined to call our crisis (the event that has catapulted us back in time to confront and heal our original trauma) our "dark night of the soul". However, this experience, for each and every one of us, deserves just as much tender compassion and loving empathy as does that of John of the Cross. Whatever we choose to call it, the experience takes us to places pretty similar to some of this.

A MODERN-DAY DARK NIGHT

Neeta described her experience to me this way:

I have never felt such terror. Day and night it kept breaking through. The grief, the loss, the waste. I didn't know what anything meant any more. Everything I had trusted and believed had been torn away. If this could happen, if they could do this to me, leave me here in this place and just not care, then it has all been pointless, for nothing.

I've trusted life, believed that if you were decent and kind, did your best and tried hard to be a good person, then life would be fair. I trusted to love, believed they loved me. But now I see that the whole world is selfish, and everyone is just in it for themselves. I don't know what to think any more, except I know I'll never get over this.

I find I'll be trying to work, do my job, and this terrible wave of fear will wash over me, so strong I sometimes have to grip the table or sit down to steady myself. Nothing has any meaning; I don't know how to get out of this. It's like the rest of the world is just getting on with life, and I'm caught in terror so big I could drown.

There's no joy; nothing to hope for or look forward to. Just this cold, heartless, unforgiving world. And nothing at the end of it all. Nothing. I don't think I can get through this. Who am I now? Why am I even here?

Neeta came to me when her family chose to take the side of her brother, their favoured son, after she had plucked up the courage to disclose to them that he had sexually abused her throughout her childhood. Their denial of her suffering was the final catalyst in a long history of denial of her suffering at the hands of her brother, a tyrant of a father, and a mother so fearful of social judgement that she had abandoned her daughter many times throughout her life. The last straw had been when Neeta's children had disowned her, choosing the comfort of belonging to the wider family over loyalty to her.

While many of us might not be able to put this experience into words as clearly as Neeta did, we will nevertheless have all experienced times similar to what she describes. It may have been through experiencing the loss of a loved one, illness, betrayal or a relationship breakup. Sometimes it's through the discovery that we have been responsible for another's suffering or have failed someone badly. It can even come about because we are disappointed in our self, feel we have seen a part of our self we are deeply ashamed of; or because something has happened that we feel we can never put right. Whatever that crisis is, it will always be a catalyst, throwing up a stream of realizations, a degree of clarity, that we have never appreciated as starkly as we do right now.

POCKET REFLECTION

Take some time to reflect on the new information in this chapter.

What feelings has it brought up for you?

What memories did you find coming to the surface? What associations did they have with each other?

What crisis has brought you here?

Can you describe its effects? Its impact?

Is it part of a pattern, a general set of themes? Like that experienced by John of the Cross? Or Neeta?

What original trauma does it repeat? Or retrigger?

Don't rush to put it away, there's no hurry and no need to do that. Just sit with this, share with your Healing Journal. Allow time for your Soul Signature to speak to you. It has such wisdom to share. Such a depth of knowing. Write down anything that's falling into place. Honour every feeling that arises.

> Give yourself plenty of time. Not only to think, but also to feel. In order to heal we need to feel. Don't fall for the spiritual bypass. It all counts. Everything is relevant.
>
> Nothing is accidental in this process. If it's coming up, then it holds a gift for you. Give it time to emerge.

REGRESSION AND OUR POINT OF PAIN

One of the things you might find happening at a time of crisis is that you feel the full impact of the original experience all over again. It can be a bit alarming if you're not expecting it. It can be pretty powerful and bewildering. Remembering these truths will help:

- All current pain is memory pain – this isn't happening now; you're remembering what it felt like then.
- Your current self is watching a younger version of you – but you're not that you, you are this you. Watch the movie, don't jump into it.
- You are not the you that you were back then, but rather the latest, cutting-edge version: you know more, are older, you have survived beyond what happened, and are wiser and stronger. This moment is different to that moment, just as you here now are different to you back then.
- Stay grounded in your body and make sure to keep breathing out – your breath is your anchor, don't hold it, or take shallow breaths. Keep the breath flowing.
- Nothing is going wrong here. Just allow the healing process to happen – where you are now, we all have been. Feel the energy. The Oneness. The love and acceptance that surround you.

- Go beyond the illusion of apparent reality – you are flowing within the stream of energy that is everything; let it hold you. Carry you. You don't need to fight it, or struggle. Lie on your back and float.

Regression is challenging territory, for sure. It can feel a bit like going mad. Here we are, a grown-up, behaving in ways that horrify us, startle us, seem to make no sense. While it most often happens at times of crisis, regressing – which is really another way of understanding "being triggered" – can happen anytime and take us completely by surprise.

> "What we do have control over, and this is far greater than you might think, is our own response, behaviour and choice. That's the path.
> That's the gift."

I recall an incident several years ago when it happened to me. I'd recently received an old black-and-white photo from my only surviving uncle, my father's brother. It was a few months after my father had died, so everything was still raw. And alive. The photo he sent me was of the farmhouse where I'd been brought up. You read the main bullet points of my story on pages 82–4, but I had a lot of memories and feelings going around inside, not all of them conscious. And certainly not all nice.

My partner, Nicky, happened to be wearing a particular jumper. For some reason – totally out of character with the adult woman I knew myself to be – I became convinced that it was one of mine and that she had taken it. I mean, really convinced. And again, bewilderingly, I was livid. So full of rage I could have wrestled her to the ground and made her give it back. You notice how childish regression is? How beyond logic, how all-consuming?

Nicky is a wise soul. She saw it all without my needing to say anything. She also knew – bless her for this – that in that moment I was in the grip of something so huge, so catastrophic, that I had lost all ability to observe or be rational. She simply asked me what I'd got going on. And in that moment, the volcano erupted. Not, as I'd feared, with red hot lava and flames and ash, but with sobs. Grief so deep I could barely get my words out. And, as Nicky followed up by asking me where I was, how old I was, what I was caught in, those tears began to give way to shivering, and I knew!

I'm a younger me and my grandmother has just died. The grandmother who'd brought me up for the first three years of my life after my mother died, before the other woman brought a chill to my world, determined to break all bonds with the past, because my father had married her now and this new world was to have no reminders of the old.

And, as I get closer, second by second, to what this is, what the jumper represents, what's got triggered, I find myself sobbing, trying to explain what happened to the girl I'd been back then. That last visit to my grandmother, who knew she was dying. The tears, the love expressed, and the cold that gripped as she'd said goodbye. Saying, "See you soon", instead of the normal "Goodbye" – as if changing that leave-taking word could somehow delay the inevitable by refusing to acknowledge it.

And then, getting home and discovering her handkerchief gripped tightly in my hand. Sleeping with it still in my hand and afterwards, for several nights, with it under my pillow, before hiding it.

Knowing I had to hide it.

And then the day I'd found that the woman who'd brought the chill had gone through my things and taken it. Knowing yet being unable to do or say anything. Wanting to scream and shout and do murder, just like now—

The jumper! The jumper is the handkerchief, and my partner is the woman who destroyed it.

That's how easily regression happens. It's the full recovery of a traumatic memory which we re-experience so intensely that it's as if it's happening right now. As if there's been no time in between. A merging of "in here" and "back then" so intense we could lose our self in it. And unless we can identify what it is that's just happened, and what we're reliving, where we're living, it can feel like we're losing our grip on reality. It spills over into "out there" too, and we find that we're seeing everything – and experiencing everything – in our life through the lens of the moment that became frozen in time. Like a freeze frame in a movie, which then dissolves into the scene where we watch an earlier event in the character's life. And through which we come to understand another layer, a hidden depth, we hadn't known was there. And suddenly we understand more. Can experience greater compassion. Maybe even forgive …

"Reach for that now, gentle soul in pain. This is your moment."

POCKET REFLECTION

Take some time to catch yourself up with all this. Call to mind earlier times that you've been reminded of. Times when you've been triggered. When you've found yourself regressed. Haven't known what was going on.

Painful times. Overwhelming, maybe. Perhaps they've even been responsible for hurt, damage? Could be that there are regrets attached to them? Maybe a wishing that you'd understood more, could have done things differently?

Conversations you wish you could go back and have again?
Explanations you could give, where at the time there were
none? Things broken you wish you could mend?

Let all that's coming up for healing flow through you. You
can do this. If you couldn't, you wouldn't be here.

Go gently and take all the time you need.

THE DOMINO EFFECT

Another helpful piece of insight that arises out of something like
the "jumper incident" is our tendency to act out "transference".
Transference is the process by which a current person, group
or situation becomes overlaid with a person, group or situation
from the past. Another example of "in here, out there, back
then". In my example, you'll remember, Nicky became my
stepmother taking what was mine (the jumper/handkerchief)
and my emotions in the transference – as I cut-and-pasted a
situation that had happened years ago onto a situation here
and now – were the very ones I'd originally experienced. It's
interesting, though, isn't it, that the memory didn't relate directly
to my father, but to a different death – that of my grandmother?

Herein lies yet another useful piece of the jigsaw. Or maybe
a better analogy might be a set of dominoes. When we set
up a domino run, all we need to do is touch the first domino,
and that domino sets in motion the process whereby every
other domino will eventually fall down. That's exactly how our
memory and the associations it holds in its filing systems work.
All that matters for a memory to be triggered is for it to stand
somewhere in that domino run. That is, all that's needed is for
there to be enough similarity between one event and another,

one person and another, one situation and another, for them to end up in the same domino run.

The domino run is not unlike the synaptic pathways that hold our memories, whereby everything links up through association. Even a vague similarity gets that memory into the domino run. And, as anyone who's ever watched in awe at a really complex domino run being set in motion – with new but related runs being set in motion along the way as the original run follows its course – will know, the further it goes the more links, and the more activities (associated pathways linking up) get set off.

THE BEAUTY OF TRIGGERS

Triggers work just like a domino run, as does transference. The apparent similarity may seem slight – maybe a word, a tone of voice, a facial expression, someone's build or colouring. But no matter how slight the initial similarity might seem, once that domino run gets underway it will unearth feelings and associations that will amaze you. And shock and appall you. And shame and embarrass you. Isn't the complexity of this journey truly staggering?

But that very complexity, and the efficiency of that domino run to find every single connected pathway, is part of the adventure of healing. I say "adventure" because I really do want to encourage you to appreciate how magnificent you are to have negotiated your way through all this, and to have got here. Take a moment to absorb that truth. All you've been through; all you've experienced and known – and survived – down the years. All those intricate layers of defences that have kept you safe from the most intolerable pain until such time as you were ready to heal it. By heal it, I mean invite it back in to join the rest of you.

Try not to push these moments away; resist the impulse that arises to do so. We naturally want to hold them at arm's length.

They're often parts of us we'd prefer not to acknowledge. Or even look at. Rather, consider them with compassion and forgive them. Hold them in a loving gaze, let them come closer. These shadows, echoes, have been unloved for years. They're hidden amongst the rubble, buried or half buried, along those three roads we talked about: shame, fear and rage. Bring them fully into the light now; they don't need to be hidden anymore. You get it now. You understand them better now. You can dare to let them come close. Snuggle them in, hold them tight. These lost and unloved parts. They have done their best to protect you by staying out of sight. Let them come home.

> "You will discover that it isn't you who has feared *them* but rather *they* that have feared they would never be accepted by *you*."

THE INNER KEEP

Shadow work – getting to know and accept and integrate the bits of us we'd rather deny or disavow – isn't easy. We're so hardwired to react with shame, fear, anger and avoidance. But that's always the way when we've forgotten Oneness. When we see ourselves as separate, and endlessly compare ourselves with everyone else. We show the false self we've constructed to the world in the hope that the world will never see the real version. And by doing so, we perpetuate the myth that everyone else is more lovable than we are. More sorted. More perfect. Just more.

Unless we allow our shadow parts back in, we can't heal, because we won't be whole. Wholeness means integration. In my own psychotherapy training and practice, a Jungian appreciation of the importance of the shadow has played a central role. While Jung originated the concept, more recent proponents of shadow work – in particular, Michael Brown in *Alchemy of the Heart*, Debbie Ford in *Dark Side of the Light Chasers*, Deepak Chopra in his book *The Shadow Effect* and Robert Augustus Masters in his beautiful books *Bringing Your Shadow Out of the Dark* and *Emotional Intimacy* – have focussed less on the theory and more on the practical application.

It's helpful here to think together about how shadow work relates to all we've looked at so far. Let's begin by understanding better what the shadow is. I often invite clients to think about it as being a bit like a huge walk-in safe, hidden away in a vault. Its walls, floor and ceiling are constructed of multiple layers of strong, impenetrable material, and the safe door itself has multiple locks, each with separate codes and combination locks. It's meant to never be breached; its contents must never be revealed or known. Sometimes, I might use the metaphor of a fortress, set behind a series of defensive walls designed to keep out the enemy: Truth.

"Truth sets us free, lovely one. Let it in."

The shadow is that walk-in safe set in the vault; it's the castle keep defended by layer upon layer of thick walls. And it takes the Crisis, and the complex domino run that it sets in motion, to begin a sustained assault on those walls and eventually knock them down. That's not quite accurate: by the time that domino run reaches the walls of the inner keep, we're usually ready to surrender. The last leg of the process generally takes care of itself.

Where does the shadow begin? Or more accurately, when do we begin putting parts of us out of sight, into the shadows? How do we create the shadow? And why?

The shadow is a container into which we have put everything we don't want to feel, remember, think about again or even be aware of. Some might associate it with the unconscious, the stream which holds all forgetting and every possibility in potential that has ever been. However, what distinguishes it is the quality of its defences. Rather like the inner keep of a castle, it's designed to be impregnable. Only a prolonged siege, a lengthy onslaught from which there is no relief, involving suffering so protracted that eventual surrender is inevitable, will break through the inner walls. The Crisis – or "Dark Night" – is such an onslaught.

The shadow is there at our incarnation, but its construction and fortification, thick walls and strong padlocks, are put in place in earnest from the moment of our Point of Pain – the original experience, early in our life, which created the wounds that we will spend a large part of our lifetime exploring in different ways, and which we will ultimately seek to heal. Its presence has been invaluable; without it we wouldn't have survived. Until now, it's housed every single aspect of our personality and experience we weren't yet strong enough, brave enough, or sufficiently equipped to face. But then, the Crisis comes, and we find ourselves under siege.

We're going to explore the shadow – and do some shadow work together – in far more detail and depth in chapter 6, The Invitation. For now, what feels important is an acknowledgement that the siege has begun and that, far from being hostile, its intentions are kind. In this siege – which is about our Soul Signature gradually supporting us in breaking down all those walls of resistance we've built up over the years – there is liberation, not capture. Forgetting is going to give way, ever so gently, to remembering. The first domino in the domino run, if you like, has just clattered into the next. The process is underway.

THE BROKEN MIRROR

There's a further thought I want to share with you. It will add yet another layer of understanding and help you to work out where your story fits into a much wider story. There's a wonderful book,

The Uses of Enchantment by an Austrian psychologist, Bruno Bettelheim, which was enlightening to me in my training, and which has continued to influence my thinking since. I've come back to it here in the context of stories, our personal stories, our family stories, our generational and intergenerational stories. Bettelheim took the essence of a variety of well-known fairy tales and interpreted them on a far broader scale, in order to demonstrate the way we manage the contents of that safe or inner keep we've been talking about through the telling of stories. Especially through the monsters – and monstrous happenings – we meet in fairy tales.

"In reality, the parts we fear the most are those in most need of love."

Pondering some of those things again, in preparation for this book, I realized there was yet a further layer still. In coming to see how everything is a story, because everything is based on illusion, energy vibrating and creating apparent reality, I gradually understood just how many stories within stories we create. Let me illustrate what I mean by exploring the tale we know as "The Snow Queen" by Hans Christian Andersen. You will probably know it already but, if not, here's a brief synopsis.

It's about the friendship between a young Danish girl, Gerda, and her little friend, the boy Kai. The devil, in the form of an evil troll, has made a magic mirror which distorts the appearance of anything reflected in it. It shows only ugliness and evil, transforming anything beautiful or good in its reflection. The trolls try to carry the mirror up to heaven, in order to make God and the angels look ugly too. But they laugh so much in the attempt that they drop the mirror, and it smashes into pieces. The splinters are scattered, and get into people's eyes and hearts, freezing their hearts into blocks of ice and distorting their vision so that everything they see looks ugly and evil.

Gerda and Kai have grown up next door to each other and are devoted friends. Gerda's grandmother tells them the story of the Snow Queen, whose kiss causes forgetting and numbness. One day, a piece of the mirror gets into Kai's eyes and heart, and he becomes aggressive and angry, ripping to pieces the roses he and Gerda have grown and tended together.

He is picked up by the Snow Queen on her sleigh. She kisses him twice: once to turn his heart to ice, and then to make him forget Gerda. The story is long; suffice it to say that Gerda goes in search of Kai, eventually arriving at the Snow Queen's palace, where she sees Kai trying to solve a puzzle made from ice. If he can solve it, the Snow Queen will let him leave. Gerda weeps warm tears of love on him, which melts his heart, enabling him to remember her and all he feels for her. Kai bursts into tears, which dislodges the splinter from his eye. They dance for joy, scattering the fragments of ice, which fall down and spell "eternity". They return happily to the village, and everyone celebrates their return.

It seems to me that this story is very relevant to the journey of forgetting and remembering we are making together here. What an amazing allegory it is! How profound and wise. The part of the story I want to focus on now concerns the mirror, which is broken into pieces and scattered across the world. In this story, it's a distorting mirror; it shows only ugliness and evil. It seems to me that it is a near perfect metaphor for all we experience in this playground we call Earth. It's a reality – an illusory one – where everything is both portrayed and experienced in a dualistic way: good versus evil, beauty versus ugliness, rich versus poor. One belief system set against another; one race against another; West versus East … we could go on.

But I reckon there's another aspect to it, which has to do with Oneness. The journey as being not only an individual one, like that of Gerda, but a journey made by every member of our Soul Family who has incarnated for this shared adventure. Not all of whom have incarnated within our immediate family, but who have nevertheless incarnated to offer us the gift of challenge and growth.

Over the years, I've noticed that there tends to be not just one individual story belonging to only one person as part of our growth, but a set of stories experienced by various individuals in different yet related ways within the same Soul Family down the generations. Each time that it's played out in a slightly different way it adds a further dimension, another layer of experience, an added perspective. The way it interweaves is intricate and complex and makes me think again about the research into life between lives we looked at earlier. Remember how we talked about how Soul Family groups go over past lifetimes together and look at how certain past experiences can be replayed and experienced from different people's points of view? Not only that, but how different outcomes can be explored, or the results of alternative choices or actions? This is very similar to what happens during a lifetime on Earth with members of our Soul Family. I'll try to show you what I mean.

"This isn't our journey alone. When we heal, everyone heals."

Let's say that certain members of a Soul Family have come to explore forgiveness. They want to better understand the causes, the impact, the consequences and different outcomes of forgiveness, and how it can have both positive and negative effects. It's likely that the various members will each encounter several twists and turns, experiencing the subject from various different perspectives, which will in turn have consequences and impact on other family members in ways that will deepen their own understanding. Everyone has a different piece of the mirror, reflecting different aspects of the experience back to each other.

We, too, get to see different aspects of the same experience by picking up – or encountering – various pieces of the broken mirror. Each one is incomplete, but each time we come across a new fragment, the jigsaw – just like the one Kai was trying to put together – becomes a little closer to completion. As a therapist, it never ceases to amaze me just how many different fragments – pieces of the broken mirror that, when put together, reflect the whole – we get to experience in a lifetime. But that "whole" is beyond one person to fully explore and experience. It takes a Soul Family to do that.

ONE MIRROR, MANY FACETS

Let's pause to take this in for a moment and ponder the enormity of it. What this means is that, while we come here to experience our own chosen journey, we also come to be a willing player in everyone else's journey too. We each hold different pieces of the same mirror, with different members of our Soul Family each offering other members the opportunity to look into a different fragment of the looking glass. Between us, we get to experience the same shared story from multiple angles.

So, if we go back to Neeta, we see that Neeta's story appears to be one of abuse, abandonment and betrayal. That's her story, so it's the one she tells. Exactly as she came to do, Neeta has fully identified with her human character, and completely immersed herself in her human personality. However, if we watch the complete movie, we see other stories, parallel stories – subplots in Neeta's movie but main plots in the movies of each of her fellow Soul Family members. For example, we see that:

- Neeta's brother was sexually abused by a cousin and was often sent away to stay with that cousin's family, despite protesting.
- Neeta's mother had been ostracized by her own family for marrying for love rather than agreeing to an arranged marriage.

- Neeta's mother had leaned on Neeta's brother because her husband squandered the family income and she feared being destitute and left with nothing.
- Neeta's children felt betrayed by her because she was so preoccupied by what had happened to her that she failed to give them the attention they needed.
- Neeta's daughter experienced her mother as being jealous of her, conflicted that her daughter could go into adult life free from all that Neeta had known.
- Neeta's father squandered money to try to compensate for his father never having approved of him, always comparing him unfavourably with his older brother.
- Neeta's brother received the same treatment at the hands of Neeta's father, who acted out unconsciously everything he had experienced with his father toward his own son.
- Neeta's brother was acting out many different hurts when he abused Neeta.
- Neeta regularly blames her children for not loving her enough, repeating the actions of her own mother toward her.
- Neeta's son feels hurt and wronged because Neeta now seems to tarnish all men with the same brush.

And we could go on. The ripples would never end. We would discover so many lives affected by the various pieces of this broken mirror. And that is the way we experience, struggle through, become engulfed in, begin to notice, process and eventually come through the stories that make up our Soul Journey as we tread our Soul Path.

Once you become aware of the way this plays out, it instantly gets easier to recognize and appreciate the gift of experience instead of focussing on hurts inflicted and wounds sustained. Seeing it in any other way is to be still living the distortion that arises when we look at the reflection, rather than looking through it. Beyond it. Most of us, if we can let our heart soften sufficiently, are able to begin to understand that those who have hurt us have also been hurt.

However, it takes a further leap, a softening much greater than that, to begin to be able to appreciate an even bigger picture still. That picture? It's the one that we can only see when, like Kai, not only does the ice in our heart melt, but when we also allow tears to wash the sliver of that distorting mirror from our eye. We have to reach a place of seeing clearly. To surrender the keep. We have to hear the voice of our Soul Signature. We must remember.

POCKET REFLECTION

Take some time to reflect on the parts of this chapter that have made an impact on you. What have you felt while reading?

What has felt comfortable? Familiar?

What has felt less comfortable? What have you wanted to challenge? Resist?

What parts of your story are you wanting to hold on to? What are you not yet ready to let go of? Or to change?

What might this tell you? Bear in mind especially those three roads we talked about previously: fear, anger and shame.

What different parts of the broken mirror might others be holding that might give you an additional perspective?

Can you let yourself look?

> What do you see?
>
> Can you hear your Soul Signature? It's present in the sensations in your body. Let it anchor you, help you find calm. Notice the breath. Feel the energy it carries flowing through you. Truth brings peace.
>
> What is it inviting you to remember?

We do the best we can with what we know, from where we are at the time. When we know better, we can do better, but only because we're no longer where we were. Never let hindsight trick you or rob you of your peace. Nothing has ever been going wrong, gentle soul. Even now, no matter where you find yourself, no matter what is arising in you, nothing is happening by mistake. You are exactly where you need to be. Take your time. All is well.

LOOK INTO A MIRROR IN YOUR SACRED SPACE

Using your word or phrase of power and intention, come into your Sacred Space. *Be here now.*

Reconnect with the energy of this place, using your breath. Breathing in, be aware of the Oneness that is everything; as you breathe out, notice that you are the breath and that you are being breathed.

Take a little while to settle into the peace and wellbeing that you always find here. Let it hold you, fill you.

Now let awareness grow, become fully present. There is nowhere but here; nothing but this.

You begin to feel heavy with tiredness. Your eyes need to close. Give in to this. You know by now that you can trust whatever this place wants to show you.

It is as if you are sleepwalking, but your body is not moving. Your consciousness is taking you along a path or passageway within this sacred space that you have created. Make the pathway as you wish; this is your creation.

As you walk, you are aware of other pathways or corridors off to the side. You decide to go along one of these. You realize you are walking toward a light. A glow. And as you come closer to that glow, you see in front of you what looks to be a small structure. A small table of some kind. But someone has built this; it is not a natural or accidental feature.

You realize with surprise that this is an altar. Similar to yours, yet not the same. It has different items – clearly symbolic – placed upon it. You approach respectfully.

It's clear that this place must hold great meaning. There are photos, personal items, some belonging to a child. Some family photos too. All draped with decorative ribbons, as if there has been a celebration of some kind.

Your foot touches something cold. A little sharp. You look down to see a fragment of broken mirror. Again, there are ribbons on the ground next to it. Celebration again.

You bend and pick up the fragment. A sense of anticipation, of excitement, begins to fill you. You know by now that this always means that your Soul Signature is communicating with you. You know you must look in this mirror.

You raise it to your eyes and catch your breath. Somehow you know that the face you find yourself looking at is also the face of the owner of this altar. Yet the face in the mirror is one you never thought to see in this sacred place. It is the face of someone who has hurt you. Caused pain and deep wounds.

You feel a strong compulsion to look away, but your Soul Signature reassures you. You need to continue looking.

A powerful energy floods your body, filling you with a stillness that takes away the fear and revulsion you were feeling. Your Soul Signature urges you to keep watching.

In the mirror, you find you are now watching this figure moving in a different setting. You watch as they speak with someone who is clearly offering them guidance. Preparing them for something. They seem to be nodding, as if agreeing to something the guide was checking out with them.

Then the view widens out and, with a shock, you see yourself. You are different – shimmering, luminescent – but nevertheless recognizable.

The person you saw in the mirror appears to speak to you, holding out their hand. You watch yourself walk toward them. There's no fear in your body language; you are clearly familiar with this person. Fond of them. You trust them.

You watch as you take their hand and squeeze it. A recognition of something. A permission. You know this is momentous.

And then, the picture begins to fade. You find yourself back in your Sacred Space, waking as if from sleep. But you are holding the fragment of mirror in your hands.

You sit holding it for a long time. Pondering what you've just seen. So many emotions are going through you, but the energy of this Sacred Space is reassuring, compassionate. You feel an embrace surround you, holding you close.

And suddenly, tears come. But they are not angry tears; there's no resentment or bitterness in them. No blame or accusations. They are tears of compassion, empathy. *Finally* a different way.

You feel drawn to look again into the mirror. You see yourself reflected back. Yet not this you. What you see is the shimmering, luminescent self that you saw in the scene you witnessed earlier.

Then you make a decision. You get up purposefully, walk toward your altar. Without hesitation, you make space for the mirror fragment amongst all the other sacred objects you have placed there.

When you are ready, take your leave of this place and come back to now. Take plenty of time to re-orientate yourself and go gently. Give yourself whatever it is you need.

Share your thoughts and feelings with your Healing Journal when the time feels right.

POCKET TAKEAWAYS

- The Crisis is the point at which an event breaks us open and invites us to heal.
- The event that does this is one that repeats our Point of Pain and makes the original traumatic memory live again in our whole being.
- It feels like re-living the old pain as if it is happening now.
- The re-emergence of our childhood pain can make us regress to (i.e. fall back into) old behaviours and childlike responses to current experiences.
- We lose all sense of what we thought we knew and who we believed ourselves to be.
- Our defences can no longer hold this back, and all we can do is allow the process to break us open.
- The Crisis is always the experience that leads to healing.

WHEN YOU HAVE FORGOTTEN...

We had thought this was over. That there couldn't be any more pain as bad as that first pain. Life had felt on track. We'd believed we'd found ways to stay safe, to get through unharmed. And yet now this!

WHEN YOU REMEMBER...

But from somewhere deep within, there came a voice, calm and certain, whispering, "You can do this. You came for this. Allow yourself to break open. Everything you need is inside you."

6

THE INVITATION

Opportunity: life presents us with the choice to
heal or to continue as we are.

"It really is in your hands, lovely
one. Everything follows from this.
Will you reach out?"

Finally, then, we arrive at the Invitation: this is the moment of choice, the stage this entire process has been leading toward; the moment of allowing yourself to break open and surrender. Everything so far has been preparing you for this.

The Invitation? To deal with your pain once and for all; to finally allow yourself to break open and heal; to let go of your projections and stories and embrace compassion for yourself and others; to step into true Oneness in the full knowledge of what it means to reconnect with your Soul Signature.

Let's begin by looking at exactly what accepting the Invitation to let yourself heal and reconnect with your Soul Signature entails. Where it fits in the journey; how it builds upon every step you've trodden so far. Revisiting the analogies of the mirror and the holograph, and the depth of meaning this profound experience of becoming human is offering you, will help to put this stage in context.

Remember the beginning, setting out? The longing? The sense that something wasn't right, yet not knowing what that something was? A series of synchronicities leading you to begin a search for answers. And for healing. Then coming across this book, as part of your search for healing. Remember all our conversations, those times of sitting side by side on the journey, taking a bit of time out to touch base now and then? Starting to hear the voice of your Soul Signature? The broken pieces of mirror gradually coming together, fragments of happenings in time and space leading you back to flickerings of awareness. Of remembering. And those times where you found yourself caught up in the domino run, reliving and retriggered? Remember working through all this and coming out on the other side? Finding your strength, surviving? Those moments of calm and relief as another jigsaw piece slotted into place ...

And now here we are. So close to letting the light in. Feeling its warmth. Its illumination. Realizing that you have been that light all along.

Marianne Williamson, author of *A Course in Miracles*, is widely quoted for her perceptive comment that it is our light rather than our darkness which frightens us the most. She highlights a second truth about love, which I see often in the therapy room. To paraphrase, it is this: that it isn't so much the love we didn't receive in the past, but the love we're not giving in the present, which prevents us from healing.

Two powerful observations, for sure. I would add a third, which I regularly meet in my work both as a therapist and as a spiritual coach. It's at the heart of the work we're going to do together in this chapter. I believe that, from our human perspective – full of our human shame, fear and rage – our greatest challenge of all is this: to believe that we are lovable.

I put it like that on purpose. It's so often wrapped up in language that doesn't quite do it justice. Like those naïve entreaties to "love yourself", or unhelpful advice telling you that you must love yourself before you can love someone else. I even came across someone on social media suggesting that the best way to love yourself was to give yourself several hugs in a day, along with pampering yourself with a special treat. This is the subject I get questions about more than anything else: how to love yourself. People reach out in bewilderment and despair; they don't understand what that concept even means, let alone how to achieve it.

We're actually looking at just another example of the "spiritual bypass" – a quick fix rather than doing the deep work of getting to know yourself fully. And, through this deep work, finding love and compassion in the appreciation of your connection to all that is. Your similarity not your difference. Our common humanity and our common divinity. People reach out to me because it sounds like it should be easy. A matter of a few affirmations, treating yourself, putting yourself first. Choosing you. Yet this is just more dualistic teaching disguised as spiritual self-help. Why won't it work? Because it's not about Oneness, it's about separation; it's focussed on me, not we. It perpetuates the illusion rather than healing it. It's not about connection. It isn't based upon the truth of who we really are: love and light become human for a while. Rather than walking each other home, it's caught up with racing in competition with each other to get there first.

We're not going to do that here. We've got this far; let's do the final bit of tough work together. The end is in sight, I promise you. Just one more steep hill and then we're in the valley, walking beside the stream.

> ## "The beauty of this moment, brave soul. Such beauty that the Universe itself holds its breath."

Shortly, we're going to do some shadow work together. To invite all the disowned, disavowed and unloved parts back in; allow wholeness to work its healing magic. Let's look in more detail at what pain really is, what causes it, and how we interact with it. Let's get to know pain – and our own pain – a little better. Crucially, the way in which we choose to interact with it determines what it becomes.

PAIN VERSUS SUFFERING

Most of us are afraid of pain. And of our own pain, in particular. So that's where I think we should start: understanding what pain is. It might seem obvious, but it isn't. I want to invite you to consider that what most of us think of as pain is something else: suffering. How are they different? Well, let's look at an example …

Here are two different ways of reacting to the same event. We lose someone we love to terminal illness. An incredibly painful experience to go through. But now notice the difference between these two responses:

> *Pain says*: My loved one has just died following a painful illness. It's been so hard, and right now it feels as if I'm breaking in two.
> *Suffering says*: My loved one has just died. I don't know how I'm ever going to go forward. They were my soulmate, and I'm lost without them. I keep going over and over how unfair it is that they're gone. I picture my life ahead and it's empty. Meaningless. I keep seeing all the things we had to look forward to, and I feel so bitter that they were taken from me. I envy everyone who still has their soulmate still with them.

Do you see the difference? We tend to use pain and suffering as if they're interchangeable. But they are opposites. Pain is a sensation, a feeling in the body. Intense pain involves the entire body. A client once said to me, having just lost his son in a car accident: "I never knew until now that it was possible to cry with my whole body."

Suffering, in contrast, is something we do with our pain that prolongs it. Keeps us stuck in it. Whereas dealing with pain in a healthy way involves leaning into it, becoming familiar with it. It means exploring its various components and what it's repeating or triggering. This takes courage and tenderness, and it's how we heal.

Suffering, however, is a defence against doing that. It holds our pain at arm's length, talking endlessly about it rather than facing it. When we choose the way of suffering, we identify with our pain, personalize it; make it the story of our life. We dramatize it instead of allowing ourselves to be present and conscious of the pain we are feeling. Our pain then becomes who we are, rather than something we're experiencing. And it becomes permanent instead of a temporary period of challenge and growth. When we become preoccupied with our suffering in this way, we feel little if any desire to move beyond it. It imprisons us. We become the "suffering one", invested in this ongoing drama.

"You have fought for so long. Struggled to keep these parts of you from ever meeting."

So what's the alternative? Well, if we resist the temptation to fall into suffering, pain becomes a catalyst. Instead of putting all our energy into building a tragic persona caught up in a drama of agonizing suffering, we use all the energy we could have wasted doing that in more productive ways. Life-enhancing ways. We focus on the challenge pain is presenting us with: to become wiser, more resourceful, and ultimately more resilient. Fearless. Courageous. Someone capable of overcoming adversity without becoming self-indulgent or bitter. We resist the pull of the shadow, all those old coping mechanisms that we needed once, but which now no longer serve us. We choose love.

Crucially, for our purposes, leaning into pain embraces the shadow, is non-defensive, and allows pain to move through us energetically so we can heal. Suffering perpetuates pain so that it becomes a state rather than a transformational experience; it maintains the shadow by creating yet more defences against reality. It's a little like the choice we make in general: to flow with what is, or to fight what is by insisting that it should not be.

It's helpful to make it a little more personal. Specific. In preparation, I'm going to invite you to return to that crossroads we sat by for a while, a little way back at the start of chapter 4. Remember? There are three paths off the main one; one path leading to rage, one to fear, and the last to shame. Every single one of us is drawn to one of those paths more than to either of the remaining two; and the one to which we're drawn is that which has the greatest magnetic pull for us personally. It's where our Point of Pain took us, and we've likely walked along it most of our life. We might have meandered along the others now and then, but this one will be the dominant route, taking us in our go-to direction. Leading to those familiar places we tend to revisit every time we get triggered.

I'm going to suggest we walk along them together. And I'm going to encourage you to explore them in detail. Don't walk too quickly or turn back too soon. We're looking to free you. Be aware when your defences want to clang into place, a bit like the drawbridge being pulled up at the first sign that the castle is in danger. Notice those moments but don't pull up that drawbridge; don't give in to the temptation to keep parts of yourself in the dark. Instead, our job is to invite them in. To let them finally come home. To accept them with love and compassion instead of denying them or pretending they're not there. We're talking pain, remember. And the many creative ways we try to avoid it. We don't need to judge that.

> **"They are closer now than they have ever been, those parts that must never be seen, must forever stay hidden in the dark."**

Let's go back to that crossroads, then, and become a little more familiar with those three different paths. Let's walk down each with an attitude of curiosity, not judgement. Where we're going to walk, every single one of us has walked. I'm going to introduce you to an actual person who's walking each path – unaware that they're even on a path, give them a name and identity and get to know them; see what makes them tick and how they view life, the world and other people. The specific illusions they've come to buy into.

My favoured path, by the way, is rage – remember the incident with the jumper? So we might as well start there.

PATH 1: RAGE – BEVERLY'S STORY

Beverly has been on the path that leads to rage all her life. Her father had blown hot and cold throughout her childhood. Sometimes he was interested and gave her lots of attention; at other times, he appeared disinterested and caught up with his own interests and concerns. When he was interested, he was exciting, and would promise Beverly that they would do this, go there. And Beverly would believe him and allow herself to look forward to the adventures her father had promised, anticipating how it would be.

However, it would gradually become clear that he had just made those promises on a whim; when she reminded him of all he'd said they were going to do, he would make her feel demanding, greedy, and suggest that it had only ever been a vague idea rather than a definite intention. He was someone on whom she could never rely. To this day, Beverly walks through the world feeling she must fight to make people do what she asks of them, while never trusting that they will.

Those of us who have found ourselves on the path of rage tend to:

- Be concerned with managing reality by trying to resist it
- Be taken up with asserting and protecting our boundaries and personal safety

Behaviours or situations by which Beverly may find herself triggered include:

- Anyone appearing insincere or untrustworthy
- Not being taken seriously or listened to
- Being misunderstood

- Feeling invisible
- Being let down or lied to

Parts of herself she keeps in her shadow may include:

- A tendency to want to be in control
- A resistance to authority or being told what to do
- Resentment of anyone appearing to be spoiled or doted on
- A tendency to rivalries and to being overly competitive

Positive traits that have arisen from her life experience may include:

- An ability to use anger to make things happen
- Activism and a passionate belief that things can change
- A willingness to speak out
- A tendency to protect and fight for the underdog

PATH 2: FEAR – LUCY'S STORY

Lucy has been on the path that leads to fear all her life. Growing up, her family appeared to go from crisis to catastrophe, always on the brink of apparent disaster. Everything that happened, big or small, was treated as if it were a threat of equal magnitude. Her mother would sob and her father would shout; there was rarely a day when there was no drama of one kind or another. Lucy lived in dread of the next explosion.

At the same time, Lucy learned to see the world through her parents' eyes. Because neither of them knew how to gain perspective or balance, neither could she. And since neither of them knew how to calm themselves or soothe their fears, they had no ability to help Lucy to do that either. Lucy therefore lived constantly with her body full of panic and heat and tingling anxiety. Her greatest fear was that no one – not her parents and certainly not Lucy herself – could keep her safe. Or prevent catastrophes. Or survive them. Lucy walks through the world doing everything she can to minimize danger, while always believing it to be imminent.

Those of us for whom this is the most familiar path show the following tendencies. In particular, we:

- Are concerned with anxiety and worry
- Engage in behaviours that are designed to prevent bad things from happening

Behaviours or situations by which Lucy may find herself triggered include:

- Feeling unsafe and at the mercy of others
- Situations where people are breaking the rules
- Anything involving the risk of getting something wrong
- Anyone who might disapprove or judge
- Any situation where she risks getting it wrong and being told off
- Any situation of conflict or confrontation

Parts of herself she keeps in her shadow may include:

- A tendency to be judgemental
- A conviction that something bad is always going to happen
- An inability to hope for anything good
- A belief that her worries or feelings are too much for anyone to bear
- A belief that she has to cope alone, because if she leans on anyone she will damage them
- Procrastination and inability to make decisions

Positive traits that have arisen from her life experience may include:

- An ability to see problems in advance and plan for them
- An ability to detect danger and keep people safe
- A healthy caution until all aspects of a situation are examined
- Reliability, loyalty and commitment

PATH 3: SHAME – JACK'S STORY

Jack has been on the path that leads to shame all his life. Jack's mum was a woman who was insecure and had known a great deal of shame herself. Her way of handling this was to work hard to be the centre of attention, to make sure everyone noticed her. Since this was her main preoccupation, she never understood that Jack needed attention, too. Jack found himself dragged along to meet-ups with his mother's friends and admirers, but was treated as if he were invisible. No one paid him much attention; and if they did, his mother quickly resented it and took back the limelight. However, Jack could also see that, although people appeared to be fond of his mother, they actually found her false and irritating. Frequently embarrassing. He watched time and again how apparent friends eventually lost interest in his mother, or actively fell out with her and walked away.

Not only did Jack grow up having never felt important or significant, but he also grew up feeling invisible and isolated. Worst of all, he felt somehow tarred with the same brush as his mum. He came to feel as if the way people felt about her was the way they also felt about him; and that the way they saw her was also how they perceived him. To this day, Jack walks through the world believing this is how everyone sees him.

Those of us for whom shame is the most familiar path may show the following tendencies. In particular, we:

- Are concerned with self-image, and how we appear to others
- Identify so completely with what has happened to us and the feelings this created that we believe these to be our identity

Behaviours or situations by which Jack may find himself triggered include:

- Being or feeling excluded
- Being made to feel different
- Others appearing to have it easy
- People being duped or taken in
- Someone wanting to be the centre of attention
- Not being noticed or taken seriously
- People putting him in a box or making assumptions about him

Parts of himself that he keeps in his shadow may include:

- A tendency to turn pain into suffering by dwelling on hurts
- A tendency to define himself by the way he's feeling ("*this is how I feel so this is who I am*")
- A tendency to judge and compare himself with others
- A deep mistrust that anyone could really like him
- A tendency to feel envious and bitter

Positive traits that have arisen from his life experience may include:

- An ability to see clearly and not be duped

- An ability to delve deeply and honestly into his own psyche
- A huge capacity for empathy
- An ability to stay with others' pain and difficult feelings
- Being able to tolerate another's darkness and be there with them

POCKET REFLECTION

Which of these three characters resonates with you? Do you see yourself in any of them? A different story, but the same impact and effect?

Do you recognize anyone you know in these characters? Someone significant to you? Someone who has affected you for better or worse?

What do you find yourself feeling on reading about these three individuals? Anxiety? Relief? Guilt? Rage? Fear? Shame?

Can you make sense of that? Try to link your response to its beginnings. Tenderly, with compassion.

Name some of your own triggers, shadow parts and strengths that have arisen out of your story. Do this in a matter-of-fact way, exactly like the bullet points above.

You are not the things you are naming; you are merely observing them with curiosity and interest.

PRIMITIVE GUILT

I just want to mention one of the major barriers to allowing ourselves to heal. It arises out of the way a child comes to terms with a parent's inadequacies and failures. Imagine how impossible it is for a child – in all their innocence and vulnerability – to even contemplate the possibility of holding that parent responsible for what has happened; or for how they feel. It makes a dangerous world unbearably dangerous. How do children manage this dilemma? By deciding – without ever realizing that this is a defence and not true – that it must be they, the child, who is to blame. Inadequate. Lacking in some way. A child strives to keep the adults in their life beyond reproach.

So Beverly decides, as do Lucy and Jack, that she is somehow to blame. And she must compensate for that in some way. Whatever it was in her that led to the pain, she must take control of it – or overcome it – to prevent it happening again. But always she sees the fault as lying with her, in her, and not with the other.

The greatest hurdle a client and I will have to overcome is to do with this mechanism. Before we can consider cause and effect together – without judgement or blame, but with curiosity and neutrality – we must deal with primitive guilt: the sense that we are somehow harming our parents/family or being somehow disloyal; we must let go of our sense of responsibility for protecting others. Anne Lamott, a writer and speaker with an extraordinary wit and sassy way with words, author of *Stitches: A Handbook on Meaning, Hope and Repair* and *Dusk, Night, Dawn: On Revival and Courage*, famously declared that we own everything that happened to us. She follows that up by saying that if our parents didn't want us to tell the story they should have treated us better.

The thing I love about that statement is the way she decides to free herself from that paralysing sense of primitive guilt we're talking about here. While we feel a compulsion to keep our parents – indeed, often our entire childhood – good, it's impossible for us to heal. Rather, we will be employing defences against healing, simply because we'll be trying to deny or manufacture experience rather than working with the version of reality we experienced. And, of course, if you've made it to this point, you'll already have a different understanding of the things that have happened in your life, and the players who helped to create them; you'll know that it's to do with our Soul Family offering up different pieces of the same mirror, having experiences and working it all out as they journey from forgetting back to remembering.

"You can lay this burden down, brave soul. It was never yours to carry."

Primitive guilt is one of the biggest barriers, then, to our feeling entitled to let ourselves heal. Don't fall for it. You don't need to protect members of your Soul Family, nor they you. When you look at it from a big picture perspective, that's defeating the object, rather, isn't it? You've all been extremely successful in giving each other the exact experiences you came for; let that be an end to it. And then remind yourself that this isn't over yet, because your own transformation is going to radiate out, and – as you've heard me say by now countless times – when one heals, we all heal.

WHY WE NEED TO DO IN-DEPTH SHADOW WORK

What does in-depth shadow work mean? Let's use the metaphor we've touched on a little before when talking about the castle, the defensive walls, and that most impregnable of all sanctuaries: the inner keep. Shadow work involves surrendering that secret knowledge, and letting the light in so that we can love the parts of ourselves we've wanted to disown back to wholeness. It means receiving back with acceptance and compassion all the parts of us – those personality traits, perceived weaknesses or frailties, aspects we're ashamed of, parts we try to hide or cover up – we would rather not go close to or acknowledge.

The problem with not doing this work is that, besides blocking our own path to healing, it means we project all those parts onto other people and situations instead. So someone who is secretly arrogant, but is keeping that part in their inner keep, in the shadows, will tend to have issues with anyone they perceive as arrogant. It will really get under their skin. A person who carries a lot of judgement inside them will spot it in others, waxing lyrical about how awful people are who carry such a trait.

As a therapist, I know that a client will often reveal their shame to me by telling me how much they despise weakness. Another might tell me how full of envy their friend is, how resentful and bitter; and they will have no awareness that they are sharing with me just how much those emotions trouble them.

We all do this. Even therapists. For years – and even now, if I don't catch myself quickly – I projected all my protective aloofness onto any cat I saw. I would proclaim how self-centred they were, how they used people rather than forming proper relationships with them like dogs do. Then, one day, in my second year at university, my landlady pulled me up short and took the wind out of my sails. I was telling her about someone in my tutorial group who was cold and withholding, and who wouldn't be generous or share her ideas. And suddenly – as kindly as she could, for she was a generous and tolerant person – she stopped me in my tracks by pointing out that I was describing to her exactly how I behaved. She said, "The problem is you don't really get to know people, do you? Or let them get to know you?"

And in that moment, I realized she was right. It had been right under my nose – the Universe had been offering me a mirror – and I had been oblivious. But I took it to heart, thought lots about what she'd said and tried different ways of being. I realized just how fearful of attack I was, how full of anger at any encroachment or perceived slight. I allowed myself to start noticing. I realized that, if I passed a group of people laughing, I became convinced they were laughing about me. I would feel my anger rise, and my conviction that people were fundamentally unkind would be confirmed yet again.

But I began to experiment. I decided that the next time it happened I would try a different approach: I would try to respond in a better way, rather than reacting in the old way. When the opportunity arose, I made myself look directly at the group and smile, enjoying the fact that they were laughing and having fun. To my surprise, several people smiled back at me and then returned to their conversation. It was clear that I'd been wrong: the hostility that I'd been convinced was coming from them was actually coming from me. It was such a shock; it was also the beginning of a long journey into shadow work and healing.

POCKET REFLECTION

Can you name a time when you came face to face with a part of your shadow?

Remember with curiosity rather than judgement. Don't push it away – it has something to teach you. Just allow the gift. It informs and completes you; it in no way defines you.

This time, instead of being matter of fact, see if you can allow yourself to stay with the experience in a more embodied way:

- What do you feel as you remember?
- Where in your body do you feel it?

Hold space and just be present; there's no need to rush, just be with the sensations.

Notice how you can survive the sensations if you don't fight them; and how, if you stay with them long enough, you eventually experience calm.

Can you find that gift in what you've just done? And in the original experience you have just revisited?

THE SHADOW AND MIRRORS

The shadow, then, as we discussed in the last chapter, is the place in our psyche into which we put all the experiences we've had that were too painful for us to face or cope with. We put them there in the form of parts of us we want to deny or distance ourselves from. Other people and situations serve as reminders of – and mirrors for – those aspects of ourselves and experiences we're trying not to own.

One further interesting fact about our shadow that I don't often see acknowledged is that it isn't only negative parts we put in there. We also place in our shadow the bits we aspire to but feel unworthy of, but which have been parts of us all along. Voltaire once famously pronounced that if God didn't exist it would be necessary to invent him. Why? Because we humans project onto the energy we call God all the parts of ourselves we are afraid to own. We look to God to be all-powerful, all-knowing, unconditionally loving. And we do this because we're afraid to consider – just as Marianne Williamson says in the reference I made earlier – that we might possess those attributes ourselves. It feels safer to let God be the keeper of those. Another form of duality, of separateness rather than Oneness. Yet another manifestation of the shadow.

Just as with all other forms of shadow work, our journey here involves welcoming back all disavowed aspects of ourselves.

If we're to reconnect with our Soul Signature, then this means our greatness as well as our perceived frailty or lack. Because, far from being separate from the awe-inspiring creative energy which creates and holds everything in the most loving embrace – which we call by many names, but which forgetting leads us to think of as "out there" or even non-existent – that energy is in our DNA. We're part of it, not separated off somewhere. That's shadow thinking. Human thinking. Forgetting.

> "We fear not only how powerful we are, but also how lovable, how beautiful we really are."

THE SHADOW IN ACTION

Sara lives with her partner, Simone. They've come for couples therapy. Most of the time, Sara would describe their relationship as happy. They share many interests, and similar views and beliefs. However, there are times when Simone becomes extremely critical of Sara, picking away at Sara's tendency to become compliant and apologetic rather than standing up for herself. If Simone points out that Sara is doing something Simone doesn't like, or tells Sara that she has upset her or annoyed her, Sara becomes anxious and appeasing, asking what she needs to do to make it better. She can't rest until things feel mended.

It's at this point that Simone turns into someone Sara can hardly recognize. She becomes aggressive, sarcastic and mocking. Sara describes how there is a sudden coldness about her partner, as if she is out of reach, unable to feel empathy or concern. Simone appears to despise her, finding Sara's vulnerability excruciating. Sara explains how, in that moment, it's as if Simone hates her. There is a cruelty and shut-down quality that's frightening. Once Simone calms down, she is mortified, and tearful; she then looks to Sara to forgive and comfort her.

I ask them to tell me about their childhoods. Sara grew up with parents who were judgemental and narrow in their thinking about the world. If Sara behaved in ways they didn't approve of, or expressed views or aspirations they didn't agree with, they would become cold and sulk. Often, they wouldn't speak to her for days until she capitulated or came round to their way of thinking. Sara remembers how anxious and vigilant this made her; how it could feel like they no longer loved her.

In ways that were similar but slightly different, Simone grew up in an environment where she was regularly bullied and mocked. Being the youngest, and a girl with male siblings, a bullying father and mild-mannered, compliant mother, there was no safety and protection. She was frequently reduced to tears, teased and made fun of. Her brothers had experienced bullying from their father, and now acted out with her their desire to be powerful rather than powerless. They enjoyed being able to make her cry, unable to defend herself. Simone would try to tell her parents what was happening, but her father would tell her to toughen up and stand up for herself. She would find herself stuttering and unable to make him understand. Her mother always tried to smooth things over, fussing anxiously until there was a semblance of peace.

Both women found themselves acting out parts of their shadow. In the moments when they experienced each other as parts of their past experience, they related to each other as those parts. As we explored those parts together, each of the women became more aware of what triggered them. Simone could see that the reason she so despised the behaviour she witnessed in Sara was because it reminded her of herself as a child; Sara was mirroring the part of Simone that Simone despised and was deeply ashamed of. Similarly, Sara experienced Simone's coldness as being the same as that of her parents when she had displeased them. This triggered the anxious desire to appease that reminded Simone of her own disavowed vulnerability.

Together, we found ways that these parts could be understood as old wounds that were coming up for healing. Simone and Sara worked hard to hold space for each other while they shared their individual stories and owned the parts they had long pushed away. In particular, their shame, helplessness, and vulnerability. As they did so, they found that the behaviours that had brought them to therapy gradually faded away.

THE DRAMA TRIANGLE

There's a helpful model of the pattern of behaviour acted out by Simone and Sara. The Drama Triangle, used in transactional analysis, shows the way in which we all tend to position ourselves in the roles of Victim, Rescuer or Abuser. Those roles aren't fixed; we swing between roles, adopting different positions depending upon our wounds, or what's being triggered in us. We can see this in the different ways Sara and Simone related to each other. Using this model can help hugely in noticing how we're interacting with others and allow us to begin to identify parts of our shadow we're acting out.

Reactivity – or becoming triggered – is a sure sign that parts of our shadow are active. Shadow work involves allowing ourselves to notice when this is happening. Only then can we start to acknowledge and understand those parts and allow them to emerge out of the shadow into the light.

HOW TO WORK WITH THE SHADOW
Doing shadow work becomes easier if we:

- *Practise being present*: learn to notice when you are going off into abstract thinking rather than staying with what you are feeling; stay in your body and senses, not your head. Your head will distance you from what is arising in you.

- *Learn to hold space*: try to notice what is happening from a place of compassion and kindness; these behaviours relate to the unloved parts of you. They have been waiting a long time for this moment.
- *Experience rather than judging*: allow whatever feelings appear simply to arise; all they ask is to be seen. Give them this gift.
- *Focus on the embodied experience*: register everything that arises physically and emotionally, not mentally or intellectually. Register the sensations in your body without shutting them down; simply be interested, curious. Notice what your body is doing: where is sensation happening? Can you notice its qualities? Its temperature? Texture, colour? The emotional tone of your response? If you find yourself moving away, notice what happened in your body when you did that. What happens when you return?
- *Become self-transparent*: honesty and acceptance are key. Lean in whenever you are tempted to pull away; call yourself out. Come back and look again. Notice with compassion why you want to move away; remind yourself how these parts have stayed in the dark for years. Can you bear – finally – to look them in the eyes?
- *Embrace our hurt instead of trying to deny or kid ourselves by masking it*: these experiences and elements belong to your story; they are part of what has contributed to forgetting. They have the gift of wisdom and greater resilience to offer you.
- *Practise becoming increasingly embodied*: be aware of the physical signals and sensations that tell you you're becoming reactive – get to know how your shadow communicates itself in your body. What does your disowned anger feel like? Your shame? Your fear?
- *Cultivate the capacity for stillness, using the breath, being present now*: encourage this as a general state of being. It

will help you to access the part of you that is the noticer, rather than the part that reacts.

- *Develop healthy empathy and compassion*: it's easier to hold these qualities in relation to ourselves if we develop the ability to hold them toward all beings. Eventually, compassion becomes our natural state and reactivity falls away.
- *Practise applying healthy boundaries*: do this both toward other people, and within ourselves. If we know that we won't allow others to encroach on us inappropriately, we no longer find ourselves being triggered or reacting in old ways; if we can trust ourselves to be aware of our shadow rather than acting its contents out, we can feel safe and grounded rather than vigilant and on the alert.

One helpful place to begin shadow work is to become aware of the aspects of other people that annoy us or infuriate us the most; also, the aspects that make us cringe with shame or embarrassment; or those that make us want to take that person on. The fact is, anything that causes a reaction like this in us is likely to be a part of us we're working hard to deny. To ignore or to refuse. Even if it's less of an issue now, it's likely to have been an issue once. And it wouldn't provoke such a significant reaction if we had accepted it, forgiven it and allowed it back into awareness for healing.

Signs that your shadow is coming up for healing include:

- *Reactivity*: having a disproportionate, often self-righteous, reaction to something or someone; getting lost in the drama and being unable to find balance
- *Self-sabotage*: procrastinating, playing the victim; maintaining a helpless, martyr-like position
- *Dehumanizing others*: reducing others to labels, objects, categories; adopting a superior position, separating ourselves apart from others

- *Emotional numbness*: becoming immune to feelings, both positive and negative, in an attempt not to experience the unpleasant sensations of emotions being triggered
- *Exaggerated positivity*: carrying an investment in experiencing only positive emotions; a determined denial of parts of our humanity – and everyone else's; maintaining a state of superficial feeling rather than allowing the full range of emotions to make an impact
- *Projection*: seeing in others qualities we deny in ourselves
- *Transference*: seeing in others aspects of other people and experiences that are triggers for us
- *Hostility and aggression*: attacking without any sense of compassion or concern; this can be external, aimed at someone else; it can be internal, where we become excessively critical and attacking of ourselves (through our internal critic)
- *Excessive eroticism*: channelling the emotional charge we carry from early wounding experiences into a sexual activity; finding release from early pain through acting it out sexually (for example, through sadomasochistic activity)
- *Inappropriate tolerance of certain behaviours*: not reacting to others' aggressive or harmful behaviour toward us; seeking this out repeatedly; finding ourselves in damaging situations time and again without knowing why
- *An exaggerated need to please or be liked*: repeating childhood behaviour resulting from learning that things went badly when we were being ourselves; and that things went better when we did what we'd worked out other people – who held all the power – wanted
- *An inability to say sorry*: a shame response, based in the belief that our shadow parts are unacceptable and cannot be admitted; if we say sorry, we're admitting their existence not only to others but – even more painful – to ourselves
- *Using pornography as a substitute for intimacy*: our culture tries to normalize pornography; however, we

dehumanize others through objectifying them, and by dehumanizing them we avoid true intimacy and closeness. Our woundedness is acted out, rather than healed within an enriching and nourishing relationship.

POCKET REFLECTION

What did you feel as you read the list on page 186? Anxiety? Shame? Anger? Indignation?

What images came into your mind? What might they be showing you?

Are there parts of yourself that you recognized which have been hiding in your shadow?

Try not to push these away or meet them with judgement. You are meeting your pain and woundedness; meet these parts with compassion.

Breathe into them. Stay with them. They are inviting you to accept them for what they are: not aspects to be ashamed of, or afraid of; but parts that, until now, have kept you safe by staying hidden until you are ready to accept them.

You don't have to do anything more than to be with them; simply be there and resist any pull to walk away.

STOPPING THE SHADOW IN ITS TRACKS

If we practise all the suggestions listed in the above pocket reflection section, we will gradually find ourselves open to hearing the voice of our Soul Signature, because the power of our story to distract us from who we really are will increasingly lose its power.

Your Soul Signature is calling your name, tender soul. Can you hear it?

In a moment, you're going to visit your Sacred Space once more. Before you do, I want to offer you a powerful and effective tool: it's the blink. In terms of breaking an activity thread, or thought, the blink is a neuroscientific miracle! Following a protracted blink, there's a pause during which you have a moment of choice. I use this all the time when working with clients; it's especially useful in anxiety work, but also in practising mindfulness and presence.

Try it out! When you blink, you have a few moments of no thought. Everything is blank. I often use the analogy of a roundabout, with several roads leading off it. Each one is exerting its own pull, tempting you to choose to go down it. However, you know where you want to go, and just need a way to resist going down an unwanted exit. How do you do that? You simply blink two or three times in rapid succession when you feel the pull of the road you want to go past, and immediately refocus on where you actually want to go.

You can use this tool effectively in shadow work, whenever old coping strategies try to tempt you away from where you need to be.

So now, let's go within. It's time to visit your Sacred Space.

DESCEND IN YOUR SACRED SPACE

By now, you know how to find your Sacred Space easily. Breathe, become still. There is only this one eternal moment. Feel it in your body, the flow of energy that is the forever now. You are stepping out of time and space, becoming one with all that is.

Using your chosen phrase or word, which is imbued with the intention that you will find yourself in your place of safety and revelation, enter your Sacred Space. *Be here now.*

Take a few moments to acclimatize; become familiar with your surroundings in this place. Notice again its familiar sound, the quality of light, the scents and textures.

This is your safe place. Remember that there is an energy field surrounding it: inside the energy vibrates to the frequency of love. It is where you step into the Universal Consciousness. The human world of time and space is muffled and faded here; there is only the clarity of remembering.

When you are ready, look around you – until you notice some steps leading downwards. They appear to lead underground.

In your own time, walk over to the steps and begin to follow them down. Always remember that you are absolutely safe here.

Take your time; you're in no rush. Bring your awareness to the steps – notice what they're made of, how time has worn them away a little. How they are worn by the feet of thousands who have walked where you are now walking.

Let your fingers feel the texture of the walls – do you touch rock? Soil? Wall hangings? Is there a smell to this place? Is it sweet? Musty? Damp? How is the temperature? How well can you see?

As you descend further, you gradually become aware that there are sounds coming from below you. They're sounds of sadness, there's someone quietly sobbing; someone else seems to be having a bad dream. Someone else seems to be chained as if a prisoner.

Reaching the bottom of the stairs, you find yourself in an underground room. It's dimly lit, and cold. Damp. As your eyes get used to the light, you see that there are figures in there. Some sitting, some standing; some lying down, too weak to stand.

Choose which one to approach. You see a lamp hanging near you. You take it in your hand and, holding it in front of you, you walk toward the figure. As this figure becomes aware of your approach, they turn toward you. You gasp.

In front of you is the most beautiful face you have ever seen, full of kindness and love. The eyes are startling, mesmerizing. They radiate love, wisdom. The deepest knowing.

You feel bewildered. This doesn't seem to fit with the sounds you heard. You had expected to find suffering, brokenness, even illness or disease. But this person is strong, glowing, radiant.

You share with them your confusion – what were the sounds you heard? Their reply surprises you: "My child, what you heard was your own suffering, your own sadness and despair. You are here to finally let them go. Come, meet those who have willingly existed here, keeping safe the parts of you that would one day complete you. The parts that will give you back your voice, your courage, your open-heartedness. Your unique Essence."

The figure has held your gaze, and it's only now that you notice that the room has become brighter, warmer. There's a fire burning in the centre of the room, and the sounds of chatter and laughter. Several figures call you over to join them round the fire, amidst cheering, and clapping and welcoming hugs. You seem to be in the midst of some kind of celebration.

Being here feels wonderful, liberating. After you have shared food together, one by one each figure offers you a gift, a token. You realize that the gifts are symbolic. As each is offered, the figure extending their hand tells you what it represents. Each stands for a part of you that is being returned to you. Not in its old form – the shadow parts you thought you were going to meet – but transformed. Your disavowed anger becomes motivation, determination; your shame has become empathy and compassion for others; your fear has been transformed into healthy boundaries and a strong voice. And so many more. Each shadow part is transformed. Take time to relish each one as they are offered to you.

Your arms full with these gifts, you take your leave with grateful thanks, and find your way back up the stairs to your Sacred Space. You notice that the altar is bathed in a strange light; you are being invited to bring your offerings over.

Laying them all on the floor, choose what you would like to do with each of them. Take time to examine and handle each one, turning it in your hand, noticing its texture, its temperature, any decoration there may be. These are sacred objects, standing for all you have been through and survived. Where will you place them? How would you like to arrange them? Honour each one and honour yourself also.

Stay here as long as you feel you'd like to. Before you leave, ponder what you might like to explore and record in your Healing Journal.

Come back to now.

Find the time and space to write in your Healing Journal.

POCKET TAKEAWAYS

- The invitation is our moment of choice – to allow ourselves to heal, or to build our defences back up.
- It is an invitation to understand the process by which the human journey propels us toward growth.
- It is our opportunity to rewrite the story we have told ourselves about our life.
- It invites us to embrace fully the meaning of the drama we have experienced and helped to create, and the role of each player within it.
- Appreciating the intricacies of that drama, and the roles everyone has played in it, is a vital part of healing.
- Focussing on understanding rather than blaming, and taking responsibility for healing rather than clinging to the perception that we are helpless victims, frees us from suffering.
- It also allows us to reconnect with our Soul Signature and remember the immensity of who we really are.

WHEN YOU HAVE FORGOTTEN...

You haven't known how you found yourself in this place. It has arisen from a longing, a searching. An echo of another place, a deep sense that there was more.

WHEN YOU REMEMBER...

Now, at long last you understand that this was your Soul Signature calling to you. That you were setting out on a journey. That everything has led to this. That the Universe knows your name.

7

REMEMBERING

Meaning: seeing how everything is linked, has been for our benefit, and finally embracing who we really are.

"And here you are, brave soul.
Your light and love are
unstoppable."
"What a path, what a journey!
You are amazing!"

Finally, here we are, beautiful soul. This journey we've been on together has at every step been bringing us closer to this point. How brave you've proved yourself to be. What staying power you've shown. This was never for the faint-hearted, and you've proved many times over how deep you can dig and all the treasure you carry inside you.

Centuries ago, Plato coined a word which meant remembering what you've always known from before you were born, but have since forgotten. The word was "anamnesis". This journey, then, is not a new concept at all. The process of forgetting all we knew before we incarnated, and finally coming to remember, has been around a long time.

> "We exist in time, but we belong to eternity, lovely one. We emerge from eternity into time and space, and then we re-emerge into eternity."

Remembering is such a sacred process. It lifts us beyond our human interpretations and perceptions, while making sense of every one of them. We come to understand our history, all we have known and lived. But we do so now within a new context. We see through the eyes not only of what we have known, but of who we really are. A spiritual being who now remembers before and after, and all that is. In one sacred and spectacular now.

Remembering is also a sacred act; the fulfilling of a sacred pledge. And you have kept that promise, just as you were always going to do. Finally, you are ready to live in the full knowledge of your true nature; to live consciously and intentionally as the Soul Signature you really are. To become the Light Worker you incarnated to be.

How can I say that with such confidence? Well, firstly, we've travelled together for some time now, and covered some tricky terrain. Many might have turned back. You've proved your resilience, your staying power. You've also allowed yourself to be open-hearted, vulnerable, and to soften. Your story, and the fact that you've not only survived it but gone beyond it, tells me all I need to know.

"You are braver than you know, and so much wiser than you believe."

Just up the road from where I live is a beautiful monastery, Mount St Bernard Abbey. Its current Abbot, Erik Varden, has described his moving journey to "remembrance" in his book *The Shattering of Loneliness*. He describes the moment his consciousness changed. As a child he had been profoundly affected by his father's story, told at the meal table one day, of having met a farmer who was working bare backed in the sun. His father had noticed the scars on his back from being whipped as a prisoner of war. Erik became hungry for knowledge, researching tales of cruelty and torture during World War II. He wanted to understand the depths human beings can reach, both in their suffering and their lack of humanity; their capacity for appalling violence. He read avidly about the prisoner of war camps, trying to trace their origin, their meaning. To try to understand what human beings actually were, at their core, when apparently stripped of their humanity.

Then, one day, he bought a recording of Mahler's Second Symphony, known as the "Resurrection". Music can get under our skin in ways that nothing else can. Listening, and reading the accompanying texts, he found himself carried on a journey through the depths of chaos and despair – the *tohu wa-bohu*, a state of "formlessness and void" – through to a moment where the singers invited him to have hope. Before his fierce independence, cynicism or his defences could rush into place, he felt something burst inside him. He found himself inspired to "remember".

He found himself seeing beyond the cruelty and suffering to the love and compassion that could make him weep for the cruelty and suffering. The two are inextricably linked. One must lead to the other if we are to heal. And such healing lies in remembering – the anamnesis that moves us out of time into timelessness, and enables us to see the greater truth, that of eternity and Oneness. That we're all in this together, creating and experiencing. In the spiritual teacher Ram Dass's wonderful and much-quoted phrase, we are "just walking each other home".

> "Do you feel that amazing energy – magical, wise, compassionate, timeless – tingling through every cell in your body like an electric shock of indescribable power?"

We each experience that moment of invitation. For every one of us, it is different. A moment in time that connects us to eternity, inviting us to remember.

I remember my dad telling me how, the morning I'd been born, he stood in a field at the farm and suddenly knew he was no longer afraid of death. Knowing what I do now about what was about to happen to him, and that every bit of joy and hope was about to be ripped away, I marvel at his own journey. One that took him to the brink of unbearable loss through to the mischievous way he knocked over the pile of Christmas presents in my bedroom that day.

> "We are at one and the same time the experiencer, the observer and the one creating the experience, and our consciousness, brave soul, has no limits."

What journeys we travel; what courage it takes. Do we ever stop and marvel at how amazing we are? Mostly, I suspect not. But I want you to do that right now. I want you to let yourself stand in awe of all you've lived and gone through to get to this point.

POCKET REFLECTION

If you were to tell your journey to remembering, where would it start? Take some time to reflect on the various points of that journey.

Let your breathing become slower, settle into a steady rhythm. Breathe into the space you now know to be you. Go within.

Recall that journey through the eyes of a rememberer; one who can see the greater truth.

Ponder, from your current perspective, the resilience and inner guidance that brought you here.

Speak directly with your Soul Signature. The Essence that is you. Wise. Infinite. Compassionate. Your Soul Signature will have things to communicate to you. You may know these straight away; you may simply enjoy being reunited with its energy.

This is the Essence you have always been. Will always be. Allow it to fill you. A vast ocean of loving energy holds you, knows you. Is you. Just as you are that ocean yet also a unique vibrational essence within it.

> When you feel ready, now or later, share your experience with your Healing Journal.

FINDING THE PEARL

In his book *Shapes of Truth*, Neal Allen talks about what he calls "The Pearl", based on a Sufi story of a pearl without price. It's a place inside us from which we're able to see our soul; that part of us that travels through time and space, making this journey from forgetting to remembering. A place from which we cannot only observe our divinity (our connection to the Oneness that is everything), but from which we can also observe our human day-to-day living and functioning in the world through the eyes of our divinity.

You, sacred soul, have found the Pearl. And once found, it can never be lost. It has always been there. My word for it is your Soul Signature. Your unique "you-ness", with a frequency all your own, and which is immediately recognizable as you no matter where you are, who you are, or what soul adventure you happen to be on. The Universe always recognizes you and knows your name, as does every member of your Soul Family.

When I first read Anita Moorjani's book *Dying to Be Me*, I remember being puzzled by her account of recognizing her deceased father by his Essence when he came to greet her following her own death. I pondered a great deal over what that meant, just as I have invited you to ponder similar information in this book. What does Essence mean in this context? In the years since, I've come to understand more about frequency and vibration, and the nature of who we really are. That we are energetic rather than physical. That we all exist within – but also as distinct and recognizable parts of – a conscious Universe. Forever creating, expanding; and whose true nature is love vibrating as light.

WHAT DOES THIS MEAN, GOING FORWARD?

What does all this mean for you? How will the knowledge you now carry influence the way you go forward from here? Well, how about we take some time to catch up with where you are? A bit of a review. A process of realignment.

> "You are a fractal of the consciousness which creates and evolves and transforms all that is in a never-ending spiral of becoming more. Can you take this in and hold it close?"

So, how could this new awareness of yours help to shape your life in the future? Here follows an example of how it might look in practice.

LIVING MEDITATION

You are just waking from sleep. From outward appearances, to an observer who has not yet remembered, your bedroom looks the same as it always has. Externally, nothing has changed. What has changed is you.

As you sit up in bed, you are aware of doing this more slowly than you would once have done. You sit up purposefully, when you are ready, by choice. You are aware.

You notice your body moving and look at your hands; you hold them in front of you, marvelling at the complex creation you see there. You touch your face. Something inside you notices the action and registers the sensation. You look the same. These hands look like they did yesterday, and your face feels just as it did when you went to sleep. But inside, you are not the same.

You are watching, noticing, from a different place. When you finally get out of bed, you pass a mirror and look at yourself. What you see is new. You find that you are looking into the eyes that look back at you in the mirror, and then through them. Beyond them.

You remember all over again everything that you now know. It never ceases to startle you into appreciating the miracle. The magic. You allow yourself to savour this remembering. Oneness. Your connection to everything else.

You know that you are not this face, not these hands. Not this body. You remember that, for a while, you appear as this body, experience this adventure through it. But you no longer identify either with this body or this story. You are flow; pure Essence remembering.

You see the sky behind you through the window; it is reflected in the mirror. You marvel at the movement of clouds, the weather; you remember that all you're watching is also you. You see a bird flying; you watch it land in the branches of a tree. The wonder of it all makes you smile. Something joyful stirs inside you. Then you understand that this joy is not inside you at all: it is everywhere. In everything. In that bird, that tree, those leaves. The sky. And you allow yourself once more to go closer to the enormity of this: it is all you. Because it is all held in the Oneness you now know to be all that is.

"Can you feel it? The eternal I AM? Life flowing through you, and into you?"

You go closer to the window and look out. Down below, in the street, are people going about their daily tasks. You remember with a jolt that they don't all know what you now know. Most of these fellow travellers are still in a state of forgetting. They still believe that all this is real. They don't know who they really are; they're living this illusion for real.

You move in closer, realizing that you can move your consciousness, that you are no longer static. You hear snippets of conversation. People talking about politics, the state of the country; the state of the world. Someone is complaining about the queues at the till in the shop this morning; another person joins in and says how miserable the checkout assistant was this morning when they visited the same shop.

Again, you smile. There's so much love in you now. Compassion. You see the suffering that forgetting causes. You notice how those people don't yet know that the world they find themselves in simply reflects their internal world, their feelings and beliefs. You try to remember what it was like before; how it felt to be that way. To not know. You find that it's impossible. You are no longer capable of forgetting.

As you shower and dress, make some breakfast and eat and drink, you realize that you are both the doing – the experiencing – and the noticing; you are both the creative manifestor and the awareness within which all this is taking place. You sense the stillness inside you as you remember these things. You are anchored; nothing can disturb you. You find yourself smiling again as you appreciate the fun and the adventure. And then, just as suddenly, tears come, and you find yourself intensely moved, full of an emotion so deep you can't name it. An appreciation of the sacredness; the enormity. The beauty.

As you walk out of your front door, you notice how rushed and frantic the life that's happening out there feels. People are hurrying along the road, busy looking at their phones, or talking to someone through an earpiece. You notice just how diverse these manifestations of the one life force are; and how every one of them believes themselves to be separate. They are trying to survive. Striving, competing, busy defining themselves in comparison to everyone else.

You feel your heart well up and fill with kindness as you remember how that was. That place where you believed these illusions too. You can still remember the pain; the rage, the shame, the fear. You can still find the memory sensations of these in your body; a reminder. You long to tell them; but it would sound ridiculous to anyone who hadn't yet begun to remember.

You look around you. It's seconds only yet feels like hours. Time has changed too, or, rather, your experience of it. You have noticed that you can slow the passing of time at will. You can take all the time you need to absorb something, dwell on it and experience it fully. Joy rises in you as you notice the air around you sparkling and shimmering. Looking up, you see that everything is this luminous energy. You can see the intensity of the colours around you; the auras vibrating around every distinct element of this reality. People, trees, buildings.

Your consciousness becomes aware that you are being gazed at. You sense this physically, like a touch. The connection arises from a little boy. He's maybe three years old. He's holding his mother's hand; she's telling him to hurry up or they'll be late. However, even though his body is being dragged along, his consciousness is focussed on you. You're allies, each holding a secret that no one else seems to know. But he knows that you know the things he does. In the midst of all that's going on around you both, you recognize the knowing you both share. You have recently remembered; he hasn't yet forgotten. You smile at each other, give a little wave, sharing this magical moment of mutual recognition. Of celebration. A sacred bond.

"Open to it, gentle soul here on an adventure. Invite it in. It is Life flowing through you and into you. It is the sacred breath, the one heartbeat, the Oneness within which we all exist."

As you go through your day, you are aware of how constantly the Universe guides you. Speaks to you. Through the sensations in your body; through a word that repeatedly shows up; through a conversation you have or overhear; through pulling you out of time into a brief daydream that shows you a new perspective.

Driving to work, you listen to music on the radio. The piece that comes on reminds you of your grandmother. An invitation. You feel a rising up of emotion. Where once you would have pushed this down, you now allow it. You have come to trust the gift you know will come. A new insight; a healing perspective. A new wisdom settles into place.

"Can you lean into this, tender soul? Can you reach through the veil of amnesia now and touch eternity?"

You notice endlessly how you are cared for, nurtured. Protected. A moment at a junction where you could have crossed but your intuition told you to wait. An instant of realization that you know something is going to happen before it actually does. You're going about your day in constant communion with the consciousness you now experience personally, but also as everything else. It is joyful, profound. You are speaking with the Universe, and it is speaking back. The language is one of love.

You are living as your Soul Signature.

POCKET REFLECTION

Let yourself reflect on this new way of being. This new possibility.

Think about your own journey to this point. All you know now that you had forgotten. How does this change you? Your life? How do you go forward from here?

What practices do you want to incorporate into your day-to-day living that will help you stay tuned in to your Soul Signature? Connected with your Essence?

How can your Healing Journal continue to help you?

How will you continue to make use of your Sacred Space?

Commit to these practices by recording them in your Healing Journal.

QUESTIONS PEOPLE ASK

How do I live in alignment with my Soul Signature?

Learn to notice how you feel when you are in alignment, and how you feel when you're not. When you're in the flow, living in alignment, you experience joy, wonder; you notice all the synchronicities through which you are constantly guided. And you are profoundly aware of the Oneness within which you exist.

How do I accept what is?

Try to remember that everything is happening for us, and that everything is a mirror. There is always an invitation to explore, enquire, grow and become more. That's the purpose of this soul journey. If we take the actions of others personally, or resent what is happening, we're forgetting why we're here. Resist the illusion that we're all separate, doing things to each other. We are all parts of that broken mirror, pieces of the whole. Every experience is offered in service; try to embrace the growth it offers. Make the question always, "What can I learn from this? How does this challenge me to grow/let go?"

Does accepting what is mean I shouldn't try to change things I don't like?

Not at all. There's always the invitation to change whatever we wish to change. However, we do this most readily by starting to accept where we are now. Where we get lost is by resenting what is and envying where others are (which creates suffering). The challenge is to work to intentionally create the life we want, while accepting where we find ourselves currently. Sometimes this can also mean finding ways to feel more content and at peace with where we are.

How do I find my purpose?

We so often think of our purpose as being something grand, something that we're here to do that will have a major impact. And yes, sometimes it is. However, that isn't always the measure. Our purpose is to find our joy and be in the flow of what we're doing so that it feels almost effortless. When we find this place, it touches lives. Sometimes it's about what we do; mostly it's about who we are. Back to being in alignment with our Soul Signature: our authentic self, empowered and living out loud. Living our purpose arises naturally and spontaneously; it isn't something we have to "find" and "make happen".

How can I stay present?

Be aware, and keep going back to the stillness within you: it is your anchor, the centre of your being. Everything else is just noise that you can observe. You are the noticer, not the reaction or the assumption; keep questioning the illusions that constantly arise. Make intentional choices regarding your thoughts. Everything is a gift and lesson; nothing is here to test you, trick you or punish you.

How can I be truly me in my current environment?

Only you can decide if your current environment is helpful or unhelpful. If it's unhelpful – which this question implies – then there are only three possibilities:

1. You change the environment.
2. You accept the environment but give yourself space away from it.
3. You leave.

This is a challenging question, and not always easy to resolve. It helps to remember that we are always in a process, as is everyone else. We are all souls on a journey, and we must follow our path. Whatever you choose will therefore be part of the journey.

How can I protect my boundaries?

What are boundaries? Constructs that arise out of the idea that we are separate. We are buying into the fear-based belief that others can hurt us. Shame us, attack us. Make us feel a certain way; trigger us. And that this is a bad thing. If we operate from Oneness, how then is that different? Well, we remember that we're all on a journey, and that we've all experienced a Point of Pain. We appreciate that until the Crisis happens, followed by the Invitation, we're all in the stage of Adjustment. That is, we're trying to defend ourselves from further pain. Usually in unhelpful ways. Asserting boundaries – helping another by giving them feedback – becomes then an act of love rather than being fear or shame-based. It means we go about it differently. We're not only looking after our own energy; we're helping the other to move closer to their own Soul Signature. Seeing it this way enables us to behave with kindness and speak skilfully. It's simply feedback, gentle wisdom-sharing: "When you do this, this is the result; if you choose this way instead, this will result in a better outcome. If you choose not to, then I have to choose whether to stay or withdraw."

What if I forget to remember?

Then your senses will tell you. You'll notice that your energy becomes dense and heavy, and you will lose your sense of joy, peace, wonder. If this happens, go back to the practices that bring you back to remembering. Slow back down, remember the breath, the importance of being in your body. Have you neglected your Healing Journal? Your Sacred Space? Find stillness, ground yourself through direct contact with the Earth. Remember you are surrounded by the love and guidance of thousands – the veil is an illusion only. Stay with Oneness until you can feel the connection again. Nothing has ever been lost; you've simply slipped into being busy, letting the world encroach rather than speak.

How do I tell the difference between what my mind tells me and what my Soul Signature is saying?

Listen from the heart – your heart is where your essence lies; whereas your mind holds all your conditioning and it also holds your defences and your shadow. Become familiar with how to differentiate the two. There is a common illusion that we think with the mind; actually, we observe with our consciousness independently of the mind. Our consciousness makes use of our brain, just as it uses our body, but it is neither. And it is independent of both. You can empower yourself to do this by using phrases such as, "My mind is telling me this, but I choose to to/believe this … ", or, "My mind is remembering that/anticipating this, but I now choose to see those things in this way … " You are always free to choose to overrule the conditioned mind in favour of your own unconditioned essence. Practise listening to the heart and being informed by that space.

How do I live intentionally?

You live in awareness of who you really are, beyond the illusion of time, space and form. You are a fractal of the creative conscious that is constantly manifesting all that is. Jump on that wave; experience its power, wisdom, intelligence and clarity. Everything then becomes intentional; you observe your choices; you notice the Universe speaking to you, guiding you; love and compassion inform your actions. You notice when you're in Alignment with your Soul Signature because you experience that you're flowing with ease. You notice when your energy changes and you then take steps to come back into alignment. Because you know that your intention creates, you live with the expectation that things will fall into place for you; and they do. You walk through the world fully aware that your vibration is being transmitted, influencing everything around you: determining the energy and content of your reality. You appreciate and embrace experiences rather than resenting or blocking their impact. You live as a Child of the Universe.

> "You have never been born; you have merely experienced what it is to be spirit taking form in a human body. You have always been and will always be, beautiful soul."

Here are some further thoughts that will help you:

- Awakening is a way of living, not an event.
- Notice synchronicities and how the Universe speaks to you.

- See meaning in everything, since everything is a communication.
- Be present and you'll be in communion with everything that exists.
- Remember that everything is a mirror, and let this inform you.
- Trust that everything is as it needs to be: don't judge or anticipate.
- Flow with what is; don't fight the temporary reality in which you find yourself.
- Accept what is, knowing you have the power to influence change.
- Always remember who you really are – and who everyone else is too; and make sure you remember that second part.
- Remember you are a Master: you are the Universe, not separate from it.
- You are the miracle that is your unique Soul Signature; celebrate this in everything you do and are.
- Find the rhythm that works for you, the pace of living that allows your energy to thrive.
- Use your Sacred Space: visit it often, as it holds everything you've been through and everything you know.
- Remember feelings are allies, not enemies: all feelings are physical sensations; they are information and guidance. Learn to differentiate between feelings (sensations) and thoughts (the stories we build around the sensations); embrace the communication and let it guide you.
- Live as a Child of the Universe – appreciate everything as a gift and choose joy, not guilt or shame. You are intrinsically lovable, innately worthy, everything else is informed by your Point of Pain. Readjust whenever you find yourself tempted to forget who you really are.

CONNECT WITH YOUR SOUL FAMILY IN YOUR SACRED SPACE

You know so well by now how to bring yourself to this place. Breathe, become still. There is only this one eternal moment. Feel it in your body, the flow of energy that is the forever now. You are stepping out of time and space, becoming one with all that is.

Using your chosen phrase or word, which is imbued with the intention that you will find yourself in your place of safety and revelation, enter your Sacred Space. *Be here now.*

Take a few moments to acclimatize; become familiar with your surroundings in this place. Notice again its familiar sound, the quality of light, the scents and textures.

Remember all that has happened here; all that is held safely here. It is where you step into universal consciousness.

The human world of time and space is muffled and faded here; there is only the clarity of remembering.

Remember that there is an energy field surrounding this Sacred Space; inside, the energy vibrates to the frequency of love. Nothing can enter without your permission.

When you are ready, find a comfortable place to sit, preferably somewhere you can lean against and feel supported. Tune in to the sacred energy of this place that has been – and will continue to be – your inner sanctuary on this journey.

It is a space that you have created, but which now exists energetically in its own right. It is both inside you but held also by the Universe itself. You can never lose this Sacred Space, and your word or phrase of intention will always bring you here. As will simply calling it to mind.

You enter this space for healing. It may be for times of reflection; for soothing and calm; for courage and realignment. Sometimes you will simply come here to remember all that has happened here; for this space holds your journey, and your before and after. You can find connection here, receive wisdom and guidance; you will find joy and ease in this place.

But just for now, on this occasion, allow yourself to celebrate; to honour the journey on which you have embarked. Be in awe of its immensity – let yourself take in its fullest significance: the courage it took you to walk this path, to pursue this adventure. Stepping out of eternity into the illusion of time and space; the enormity of each stage that led you here.

Close your eyes for a moment, and revisit some of the key moments of the road you have travelled. Remember as you do so that you are safe here. Take in the sounds and the scents, the textures and colours; be aware of them while you let yourself recall where you have been. Give yourself whatever time you need to do this; re-open your eyes only when you're ready.

As you open your eyes, you notice that the space is shimmering all around you. The energy is one of joy. You feel the anticipation and invitation pulsing through you;

you are shimmering too. Puzzled but intrigued, you look around you. You notice the altar you made right at the outset. It seems to be drawing you over to it. There's something different about it. It's bathed in sparkling light; but more than that, the entire altar seems to be vibrating. In motion. As if it isn't solid. It appears fluid – but now so does everything else. This doesn't feel at all frightening; it's as if it makes perfect sense to you. Somehow you recognize this.

Yet at the same time, the ground beneath you is firm. As you touch the textures around you, and take in the sounds and scents, they are as real as they ever were. Just more intense; magnified.

And then it happens! The altar seems to dissolve into a vast expanse of luminosity – light so bright you find that you're looking through half-closed eyes. And yet you *do* look. You watch in awe as it transforms into an energy that seems to surround and hold you, like a blanket. Within it, you experience love so immense, compassion and kindness, such utter acceptance that you find yourself in tears. It's like nothing you've ever known – and yet it knows you completely. You feel so profoundly known that every part of your being lets go, relaxes into an embrace so deeply satisfying that everything else melts away. And you feel arising in you the memory of this. You have known this. *Before.*

Then there is a sound. You had forgotten it but recognize it now. A low, penetrating hum, like a lullaby. It is within you, but outside of you also; it fills everywhere. Everything. You feel it vibrating through your entire being. Again, it is so familiar, yet you had forgotten. And now, as it fills you, your awareness shifts again.

You feel the presence of other Essences, so close. You realize you know them but had forgotten. Your guide stands smiling and reassuring; your ancestors are here. And so many who have always known and loved you but who you do not yet recognize. Yet you feel their love. And somewhere, far off yet so bright it is impossible to ignore, a light that you know is at the very centre. It intensifies as you gaze into it: the highest vibration in the Universe. You give it whatever name holds meaning for you. And in the same way in which the flame of a candle can suddenly leap, you sense this light do the same. You are seen and known. And so loved.

A recognition. A confirmation. A blessing. On you, and on this Sacred Space.

Then, just as quickly, the shimmering eases. All is as it was. A portal into eternity. Here, in this space. *Inside you.* Available to you always.

You take time to ponder and to absorb all you have just been shown. Then, with a light step and a swelling heart, dear Child of the Universe, you come back to this page, in this book, held in these hands, and our eyes meet. We smile and bow to the journey, to each other, and to the path we have just walked together. Knowing that we are, always have been, and always will be, One.

POCKET TAKEAWAYS

- To remember who you really are is to live in the knowledge that you are forever connected to the flow that is everything.
- When you know you are connected to everything, and everything is connected to you, you open yourself to infinite wisdom and intelligence.
- You see signs, messages and meaning in everything and recognize that the Universe is constantly communicating with you.
- You allow yourself to reconnect with your Soul Signature, the fullness of all you really are.
- You live intentionally, in awareness and compassion, and see through the illusions that you find those around you still believing.
- Your light and your energy are no longer limited and you are empowered to make the difference you came to make.
- You are living your Soul Purpose, in full alignment with your Soul Signature.
- You are finally living as the Light Worker you incarnated to become.

WHEN YOU HAVE FORGOTTEN...

So this is Oneness. This is peace and belonging. This is the journey come full circle. Everything makes sense now. The deepest healing and the most liberating growth is underway. It has brought a calm like no other.

WHEN YOU REMEMBER...

We find ourselves filled with such tenderness and compassion, such generosity and acceptance. So many still walk asleep, but now you awaken, and your light shows others the way home.

AFTERWORD

Never lose sight of the fact, lovely one, that you are a Light Bearer and a way-shower.

So many times, I know, it's hard to see that. There have been so many challenges, so much fear, pain, and loss. It has felt like being shattered and broken, and you've had to dig deep to find your way out, to put yourself back together again.

But see, that is your message, brave soul. That is your story and your gift. You have found your way, walked your path, grown stronger and wiser. You have stories inside you that only you have lived.

You may not think of yourself as an inspiration, gentle soul. You may not feel you have anything unique or valuable to offer. But I can tell you that, in the unseen world, closer than a heartbeat, there are young souls eager to incarnate for the adventure because of YOU, your example, your light, and because of all you've survived. It has left them in awe!

And you have such wisdom inside you, sacred soul, from walking your path, wading through your challenges, reaching despair and surviving, touching joy and being inspired by moments of dazzling clarity and the purest love and compassion.

There is so much you have lived, so many storms and so many miracles. You have conversed with the divine and walked unknowingly with angels.

Stop playing small, beautiful soul. Truth is, you rock!

Now go and live out loud! And be sure to have some fun! Puddles, sunsets and cake – enjoy it all!

ACKNOWLEDGEMENTS

When you get an email out of the blue from a publishing house, in which someone tells you they found you on Instagram, love your work, and wondered if you'd care to collaborate in writing a book, your first thought – certainly mine – is to think they must have made a mistake and sent it to the wrong person. Either that, or it's very probably a scam.

So when the offer turns out to be real, and the interest genuine, it comes as the most wonderful surprise. I have to thank Jo Lal, who sent me that initial email, for seeing whatever it was she perceived in my writing, and in me, and for persisting till we had fleshed out precisely what the book was to be. Jo, you showed up just when life had become a little too comfortable, and I'd become ever so slightly complacent, and offered me the most incredible opportunity to grow some more! You have stretched and pushed and squeezed me, and I appreciate so much the immense faith you placed in me. Your clarity of vision and ear for tone and voice, desire to get it absolutely right, honesty of feedback and attention to detail throughout, has been so refreshing and challenging. I owe you a great deal.

One of the other great joys of working on this book has been the warmth, creativity, vision and constant encouragement of my editor, Sue Lascelles. On several occasions, when I have become convinced that I couldn't get my head around an idea, or find a way to incorporate an editorial suggestion effectively, she has chuckled, reassured me that I wasn't remotely the only author to become convinced they should just give back the advance and call it a day, and gently and with great skill convinced me to keep going. Sue has the rare knack of sharing her insights and suggestions with the lightest touch, of getting the best out of you by demonstrating her belief that you have what's needed if you just trust the process. She has a wonderful knack of finding alternative ways to achieve what's needed, and coming up with solutions when you feel at a loss. It takes someone with enormous generosity to enable an author in this way; Sue possesses that generosity in abundance. Sue, your input has been priceless, and I shall miss working with you a great deal.

When I look back at the long journey involved in becoming a psychotherapist, and the influences which helped form me, and trained me – and there have been so many – three people stand out above all others. They are Professor Michael Jacobs, from whom I learned a degree of inner calm, reflectivity and integrity, and the ability to listen to the 'still small voice' inside me, and inside everyone which has never left me; the late Moira Walker, who taught me the importance of clinical technique, the power of the spoken word, and that everything should imbued with empathy and compassion; and the late Peter Lomas, who taught me to allow and access a depth of humanity - one that recognises ourselves in the other, and the Oneness in everything – and also that we should always question, not merely accept, that I have brought to my work ever since. To these wonderful souls, I owe who I am as a therapist, and a great deal of who I am as a human being. Their generosity in sharing so much of themselves with vulnerability and openness has been such a role model for me, and has given me the courage to do the same.

This book would never have come about without the very special group of sparkly people I call my Tribe. These wonderful souls began finding me in earnest about 10 years ago when, after much reluctance and a great deal of persuasion by the younger members of the Juddly clan, I first ventured onto Facebook. This amazing soul family, which has members on every continent, and with whom I know I have walked through many lifetimes down the ages, has never failed to encourage and champion me, and I treasure their presence, their wisdom and their incredible vibes more than I can ever express in words. It has been so delicious to connect with you again for another adventure! We recognised each other so quickly, and simply knew each other by each other's energy. You know who you are! In especially loving memory, and in deep gratitude, to Carl. You inspire us still!

It feels unthinkable, also, not to express my deepest gratitude, respect and awe for all those who have allowed me to walk alongside them for a while as they found their way back towards remembering and healing. This human journey, and everything we encounter as souls whilst here on this planet, is so complex, so vast in its remit, that anyone undertaking such a journey is courageous in the extreme. I have met many such souls – clients, students, supervisees and trainees and, more recently, followers on social media who have shared questions and thoughts with me. On every occasion, I have been humbled by your stories and life experiences, your tenacity and bravery. You have been very much the inspiration behind this book.

I must also thank the growing community of followers who have encouraged me to believe I have something worth saying, and who show up day in and day out to message me, share with me, make suggestions and requests, force me to firm up ideas and find better ways of communicating them. You are an endless source of light and inspiration, and warm my heart more than you will ever know. Thank you for your astonishing loyalty and support. I look forward so much to sharing many more adventures with you!

Most especially of all, I want to thank my family and the wider Juddly clan for getting behind me, and this project, so steadfastly over the past year or so. It's not easy being alongside someone who is living, breathing, eating and sleeping the birthing of a book. I have felt held and loved, known and believed in. Thank you, Nicky, for your love and care, for making me feel so known

ACKNOWLEDGEMENTS

and understood, for your confidence and belief in me, your occasional firm words when needed, your endless willingness to read drafts and talk ideas through, deepening and extending and inspiring new thoughts, and for your patient understanding and encouragement when I've temporarily lost my nerve, and for always reminding me to listen to the tall figure we first encountered together in that tiny Derbyshire cottage, even when I'm paralysed with self-doubt; thank you, Barbara, for being such a stalwart rock and champion, and for the powerful bursts of reiki and shot-in-the-arm banter and humour, tea and cake in times of need, and for setting all this in motion all those years ago on your kitchen table. Thank you to my sons, Andy and Dave, for always being ready with a hug or a joke or a bit of common sense on the phone when needed, for all you've shown and taught me down the years, for the fun and laughter and gentle presence during difficult times, and your fierce loyalty and support down the years, and for choosing me as a mum and letting me know you're proud of me. And thank you to my daughter, Becky, one of the bravest and most tenacious souls I know, a true mover and shaker facing challenges which would be beyond most of us to bear. And thank you, Martha, Flora and Rory, Kirsty, Stacey, Helen and Pierce, for all the many ways you've shown kindness and interest, been excited to hear how it's going, and helped me believe I could do this.

And finally, thank you, Lilly and Noah, for reminding me to laugh and play and be silly, and for the gift of remembering to look at the world through the eyes of a child, and to never forget to look for the magic. For you are closest of all to remembering, and have more to teach us than we can ever learn.

RECOMMENDED READING

THE SPIRITUAL JOURNEY

Adyashanti. *Falling into Grace: Insights in the End of Suffering*. Sounds True, reprint edition 2011.

Byron, Katie. *A Thousand Names for Joy: How To Live in Harmony With The Way Things Are*. Ebury Digital, 2008.

Byron, Katie. *A Mind At Home with Itself: Finding Freedom in a World of Suffering*. Ebury Digital, 2017.

Chodron, Pema. *The Places That Scare You: A Guide to Fearlessness*. Element, 2013.

Chodron, Pema. *Welcoming the Unwelcome: Wholehearted Living in a Brokenhearted World*. Shambala, 2019.

Dyer, Wayne W. *Change Your Thoughts – Change Your Life: Living the Wisdom of the Tao*. Hay House, 2007.

Hudson, Russ and Riso, Don Richard. *The Wisdom of The Enneagram*. Bantam, 1999.

Tolle, Eckhart. *A New Earth: Awakening to Your Life's Purpose*. Penguin, 2008.

Tolle, Eckhart. *Oneness With All Life*. Michael Joseph, 2018.

SPIRITUAL AWAKENING

Allen, Neal. *Shapes of Truth: Discover God Inside You*. Pearl Publications, 2020.

Maa Jenson, Amoda. *Embodied Enlightenment: Living Your Awakening in Every Moment*. Reveal Press, 2017.

Rohr, Richard. *Immortal Diamond: The search for our true self*. SPCK, 2013.

Rohr, Richard. *The Wisdom Pattern: Order, Chaos and Reorder*. Franciscan Media, 2020.

Starr, Mirabai. *Saint John of The Cross: Devotions, Prayers & Living Wisdom*. Published 2008.

Starr, Mirabai. *Caravan of No Despair: A Memoir of Loss and Transformation*. Sounds True, 2015.

Taylor, Steve. *The Leap: The Psychology of Spiritual Awakening*. Hay House UK, 2017.

Taylor, Steve. *Spiritual Science: Why Science Needs Spirituality to Make Sense of the World*. Watkins; New edition, 2018.

Taylor, Steve. *Extraordinary Awakenings: When Trauma Leads To Transformation*. New World Library, 2021.

Varden, Erik. *The Shattering of Loneliness: On Christian Remembrance*. Bloomsbury Continuum, 2018.

Welwood, John. *Toward a Psychology of Awakening: Buddhism, Psychotherapy and the Path of Personal and Spiritual Transformation*. Shambhala, 2002.

Williamson, Marianne. *Tears to Triumph: The Spiritual Journey from Suffering to Enlightenment*. HarperOne, 2016.

THE NATURE OF CONSCIOUSNESS

Blomqvist PhD, Johanna. *Hyperreality: Beyond the Horizon where Physics Meets Consciousness.* Mindstream Publishing, 2021.

Braden, Gregg. *The Divine Matrix: Bridging Time, Space, Miracles and Belief.* Hay House Inc., 2008.

Chopra, Deepak, and Rudolph E. Tanzi. *Super Genes: Unlock the Astonishing Power of Your DNA for Optimum Health and Well-Being.* Harmony, 2017.

Chopra, Deepak. *The Book of Secrets: Who Am I? Where Did I Come From? Why Am I Here?* Ebury Digital, 2019.

TRAUMA

Levine, Peter A. *Waking the Tiger: Healing Trauma.* North Atlantic Books, 1997.

Levine, Peter A. *Trauma through a Child's Eyes,* North Atlantic Books, 2010.

Levine, Peter A. *In an Unspoken Voice: How the Body Releases Trauma and Restores Goodness.* North Atlantic Books, 2012.

Levine, Peter A. *Trauma and Memory: Brain and Body in a Search for the Living Past: A Practical Guide for Understanding and Working with Traumatic Memory.* North Atlantic Books, 2015.

Maté, Gabor. *When the Body Says No: The Cost of Hidden Stress.* Knopf Canada, 2003.

Rothschild, Babette. *The Body Remembers: The Psychophysiology of Trauma & Trauma Treatment.* Norton Professional Books, 2000.

Van Der Kolk, Bessel & Elizabeth Stanley. *The Body Keeps the Score: Brain, Mind, and Body in the Healing of Trauma.* Penguin Books, 2015.

Van Der Kolk, Bessel & Elizabeth Stanley. *Widen the Window: Training your Brain and Body to Thrive during Stress and Recover from Trauma.* Yellow Kite, 2019.

Wolynn, Mark. *It Didn't Start with You: How Inherited Family Trauma Shapes Who We Are and How to End the Cycle.* Penguin Life, 2017.

LIFE BETWEEN LIVES

Alexander, Eben. *The Map of Heaven: A Neurosurgeon Explores the Mysteries of the Afterlife and the Truth about What Lies Beyond.* Piatkus, 2014.

Alexander, Eben. *Living in a Mindful Universe: A Neurosurgeon's Journey into the Heart of Consciousness.* Piatkus, 2017.

Elsen, Pieter Jan PhD. *When Souls Awaken: Real-Life Accounts of Past-Life and Life-Between-Lives Regressions.* Pieter Elsen, 2019.

Long, Jeffrey. *Evidence of the Afterlife: The Science of Near-Death Experiences.* HarperOne, 2009.

Long, Jeffrey. *God and the Afterlife: The Groundbreaking New Evidence for God and Near-Death Experience.* Harper One, 2016.

Martini, Richard. *Flipside: A Tourist's Guide on How to Navigate the Afterlife.* Homina Publishing, 2013.

Moody, Dr. Raymond. *Glimpses of Eternity: An Investigation into Shared Death Experiences*. Ebury Digital, 2011.

Moody, Dr. Raymond. *Life After Life*. Ebury Digital, 2016.

Moorjani, Anita. *Dying To Be Me: My Journey from Cancer to Near Death, to True Healing*. Hay House, 2012

Moorjani, Anita. *What If This Is Heaven?: How Our Cultural Myths Prevent Us from Experiencing Heaven on Earth*. Hay House Inc., 2016.

Newton, Michael. *Journey of Souls: Case Studies of Life Between Lives*. Llewellyn Publications, 2010.

Newton, Michael. *Wisdom of Souls: Case Studies of Life Between Lives from The Michael Newton Institute*. Llewellyn Publications, 2019.

Singer, Michael A. *The Untethered Soul: The Journey Beyond Yourself*. New Harbinger Publications, 2007.

Stevenson, Ian M.D. *Children Who Remember Previous Lives: A Question of Reincarnation*. McFarland, 2016.

Tucker, Dr. Jim. *Return to Life: Extraordinary Cases of Children Who Remember Past Lives*. St. Martin's Press, 2013.

THE SHADOW

Augustus, Robert. *Bringing Your Shadow Out of the Dark: Breaking Free from the Hidden Forces That Drive You*. Sounds True, 2018.

Augustus, Robert. *Spiritual Bypassing: When Spirituality Disconnects Us from What Really Matters*. North Atlantic Books, 2010.

Brown, Michael. *Alchemy of the Heart: Transform Turmoil into Peace Through Emotional Integration*. Namaste Publishing, 2008.

Ford, Debbie. *The Dark Side of the Light Chasers: Reclaiming Your Power, Creativity, Brilliance, and Dreams*. Hodder & Stoughton, 2011.

THE ENERGETIC UNIVERSE

Braden, Gregg. *The Divine Matrix: Bridging Time, Space, Miracles, and Belief*. Hay House, 2008.

Dispenza, Dr. Joe. *Becoming Supernatural: How Common People Are Doing the Uncommon*. Hay House, 2017.

Emoto, Masaru. *The Miracle of Water*. Atria Books, reprint edition 2010.

Emoto, Masaru. *The Hidden Messages in Water*. Atria Books, illustrated edition 2013.

Lipton, Bruce H. *The Biology of Belief: Unleashing the Power of Consciousness, Matter & Miracles*. Hay House, 2008.

McTaggart, Lynne. *The Bond: Connecting Through the Space Between Us*. Hay House UK, 2013.

THE POWER OF INTENTION

Braden, Gregg. *Secrets of the Lost Mode of Prayer: the Hidden Power of Beauty, Blessing, Wisdom, and Hurt.* Hay House Inc., 2nd edition 2016.

Chopra, Deepak. *The Shadow Effect: Illuminating the Hidden Power of Your True Self.* Harper One, 2010.

Dispenza, Dr. Joe. *You Are the Placebo: Making Your Mind Matter.* Hay House Inc., 2014.

Lipton, Bruce. *Spontaneous Evolution: Our Positive Future and a Way to Get There from Here.* Hay House Inc., 2009.

McTaggart, Lynne. *The Intention Experiment: Use Your Thoughts To Change The World.* Harper Element, 2008.

McTaggart, Lynne. *The Power of Eight: Harnessing the Miraculous Energies of a Small Group to Heal Others, Your Life and the World.* Hay House UK, 2017.

SCIENCE AND SPIRITUALITY

Hamilton, David R. *Why Woo Woo Works: The Surprising Science Behind Meditation, Reiki, Crystals, and Other Alternative Practices.* Hay House UK, 2021.

Kamene, Kaba Hiawatha. *Spirituality Before Religions: Spirituality is Unseen Science … Science is Seen Spirituality.* Kaba Hiawatha Kamene, 2019.

Levy, Paul. *Quantum Revelation: A Radical Synthesis of Science and Spirituality.* Select Books, 2018.

Popham, Sajah. *Evolutionary Herbalism: Science, Spirituality, and Medicine from the Heart of Nature.* North Atlantic Books, 2019.

Sheldrake, Rupert. *The Science Delusion: Freeing the Spirit of Enquiry.* Coronet, 2012.

Sheldrake, Rupert. *Dogs That Know When Their Owners Are Coming Home: And Other Unexplained Powers of Animals.* Cornerstone Digital, 2013.

Sheldrake, Rupert. *The Sense of Being Stared At: And Other Aspects of the Extended Mind.* Cornerstone Digital, 2013.

Sheldrake, Rupert. *Science and Spiritual Practices: Reconnecting through Direct Experience.* Coronet, 2017.

Sheldrake, Rupert. *Ways to Go Beyond and Why They Work: Seven Spiritual Practices in a Scientific Age.* Coronet, 2019.

THE NATURE OF HEALING

Aurand, Paul. *Essential Healing: Hypnotherapy and Regression-Based Practices to Release the Emotional Pain and Trauma Keeping You Stuck.* Reveal Press, 2021.

Blomqvist PhD, Johanna. *From Quantum Physics to Energy Healing: A Physicist's Journey to Mind and Healing.* Mindstream Publishing, 2018.

Braden, Gregg. *The Wisdom Codes.* Hay House Inc., 2020.

Corby, Rachel. *Rewild Yourself: Becoming Nature.* Amanita Forest, 2015.

Francis, Paul. *Finding Your Deep Soul: Guidance for Authentic Living Through Shamanic Practices.* Paul Francis, 2019.

Francis, Paul. *Rewilding Yourself: Discovering Your Soul's Deep Roots through Shamanic Practices*. Paul Francis, 2018.

Heuertz, Christopher. *The Sacred Enneagram: Finding Your Unique Path to Spiritual Growth*. Zondervan, 2017.

Heuertz, Christopher. *The Enneagram of Belonging: A Compassionate Journey of Self-Acceptance*. Zondervan, 2020.

Ingerman, Sandra. *Medicine for the Earth: How to Transform Personal and Environmental Toxins*. Harmony, 2010.

Ingerman, Sandra. *Walking in Light*. Sounds True, 2015.

Lad, Dr. Vasant. *Ayurveda: The Science of Self-Healing: A Practical Guide*. Lotus Press, 1984.

Maté, Gabor. *In the Realm of Hungry Ghosts*. Ebury Digital, 2018.

Maté, Gabor. *Scattered Minds: The Origins and Healing of Attention Deficit Disorder*. Ebury Digital, 2019.

Simon, David. *Free to Love, Free to Heal: Heal Your Body by Healing Your Emotions*. Chopra Centre Press, 2015.

Wall Kimmerer, Robin. *Braiding Sweetgrass: Indigenous Wisdom, Scientific Knowledge and The Teachings of Plants*. Penguin, 2020.

GETTING IN TOUCH

You can find Janny:

- on Instagram at www.instagram.com/jannyjuddly
- on Facebook www.facebook.com/ttinmypocket
- on Spotify and iTunes and YouTube as Janny Juddly, The Therapist in my Pocket

If you would like to contact her directly, you can do so using the message form on her website: www.jannyjuddlythetherapistinmypocket.com.

To work with Janny one to one, visit her psychotherapy website: thetherapistinmypocket.uk

ABOUT US

Welbeck Balance publishes books dedicated to changing lives.
Our mission is to deliver life-enhancing books to help improve
your wellbeing so that you can live your life with greater clarity
and meaning, wherever you are on life's journey. Our Trigger
books are specifically devoted to opening up conversations
about mental health and wellbeing.

Welbeck Balance and Trigger are part of the Welbeck Publishing
Group – a globally recognized independent publisher based
in London. Welbeck are renowned for our innovative ideas,
production values and developing long-lasting content.
Our books have been translated into over 30 languages in
more than 60 countries around the world.

If you love books, then join the club and sign up
to our newsletter for exclusive offers, extracts,
author interviews and more information.

www.welbeckpublishing.com   www.triggerhub.org

   🐦 welbeckpublish   🐦 Triggercalm
   📷 welbeckpublish   📷 Triggercalm
   📘 welbeckuk   📘 Triggercalm

WELBECK
BALANCE

TRIGGER™
Your Specialist Mental Health & Wellbeing Hub